ASTROLOGY
AND OTHER
OCCULT GAMES

by MARGARET and EVE RONAN

Designed by
Patricia Millichap

SCHOLASTIC BOOK SERVICES
New York Toronto London Auckland Sydney Tokyo

Tarot cards designed by Pamela Colman Smith, under instruction of Arthur Edward Waite.

1st printing ....April 1972
Printed in U.S.A.

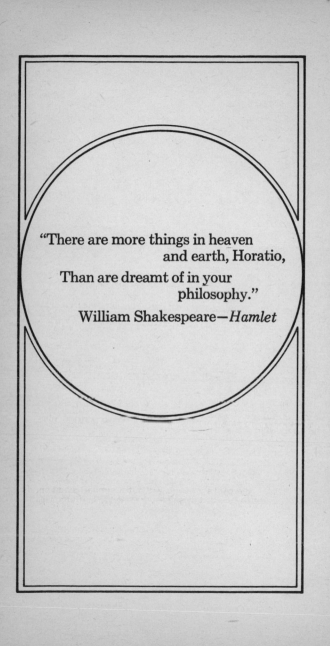

"There are more things in heaven
and earth, Horatio,

Than are dreamt of in your
philosophy."

William Shakespeare—*Hamlet*

CONTENTS

INTRODUCTION

"What's going to happen to me? Will I be rich, famous, happy? How can I make the most of myself?"

If you ask yourself these questions, you're interested in the future. You'd like to know what's ahead — for you, your family, and friends. For fun and answers try occult games!

What are occult games? They are the games people have played for centuries as they tried to peer into the future. These games have ancient names — Astrology, Palmistry, Numerology, The Tarot, the I Ching. But old as they are, they are part of today's life-style. In fact, many people say that these occult (a word meaning "secret" or "mysterious") games are really part of a new pop-science because, like science, they have certain rules and regulations that are supposed to produce certain results. Others say the occult is more superstition than science.

Silly superstition? A passing fad? A maybe-there-could-be-something-in-it key to the future? Whatever your opinion, we hope that you'll agree that the games of the occult are fun to play. You'll find the rules of these games on the following pages. If you follow the rules carefully, you'll also discover that no player loses at occult games. Whether you play for fun or for keeps, each game can help you to win new understanding of yourself.

SAGITTARIUS (impulsive, nature-loving)

SCORPIO (shrewd, resourceful)

JUPITER

MARS

LIBRA (sociable, even-tempered)

VENUS

MERCURY

VIRGO (studious, critical)

SUN

MOON

LEO (proud, courageous)

CANCER (sensitive, persistent)

HOROSCOPE

ASTROLOGY

What's your sign?

Ask that question the next time you want to get a conversation started. Whether or not they really believe in astrology, most people are turned on by the signs of the zodiac. That's why astrology magazines sell ten million copies a year, and astrology columns offering daily forecasts appear in over 1,200 U.S. newspapers.

Today astrology is a billion dollar business as well as a popular pastime. Computers cough up printouts showing what the planets and stars mean in your life. Designers, hairdressers, and jewelers offer styles to suit your sign. And if you want to let the rest of the world know what sign you were born under, you can buy stationery, key chains, T-shirts, eyeglasses, handkerchiefs, and ballpoint pens that tell the world you're a Leo, an Aries, a Libra, or a Capricorn.

For centuries astrology has been regarded as a "tool of divination" — something used to foretell the future. You don't have to take it that seriously, but don't be surprised if it helps you gain new insights into yourself and your friends. As one teenager put it: "A good horoscope makes you realize that what you do matters. It shows you that all your actions affect others, as well as yourself. It makes you see that you have a responsibility to make the right choice."

Some astrologers point out that astrology tells more about character than about the future.

"It shows us what talents and abilities we have. But the way we use these abilities is up to us — not up to the stars." In other words, your future depends on what *you* do with what you have.

In many ways, astrology is like a friend who will give you straight answers and good advice. But don't expect it to flatter you, or make excuses for your failures. It will be just as quick to point out your shortcomings as your good points.

Who Cast the First Horoscope?

No one knows for sure. The first astrologer was probably a high priest in ancient Babylon. As far back as the 6th century B.C., these priest-astrologers were making charts showing how the planets moved among the seemingly fixed stars. (The word "planet" means "wanderer" in Greek.) They also noticed that some groups of stars, called *constellations*, seemed to resemble the outlines of certain animals or people or objects. They marked off an imaginary zone of the sky that contained twelve of these constellations, and called it the *zodiac*, or "circle of animals."

Imagine the zodiac as the face of a clock. Put Aries the Ram at one o'clock; Taurus the Bull at two; Gemini the Twins at three; Cancer the Crab at four; Leo the Lion at five; Virgo the Virgin at six; Libra the Scales at seven; Scorpio the Scorpion at eight; Sagittarius the Archer at nine; Capricorn the Sea-Goat at ten;

Aquarius the Water-Bearer at eleven; and Pisces the Fishes at twelve o'clock.

To these early astrologers, the sun, moon, and the planets seemed to move through the zodiac from East to West. Anything that could move over such vast distances, they reasoned, must be very powerful — perhaps powerful enough to be gods that could control the destinies of men. After all, thought the astronomers, those strange lights in the sky seemed to have a lot to do with the way the crops grew and the tides moved. Perhaps they also influenced the way men moved and thought and acted.

The early astrologers not only turned the planets into gods, they also made them rulers of the signs of the zodiac. Venus was declared the ruler of both Taurus and Libra; Saturn of Aquarius and Capricorn; Jupiter of Pisces and Sagittarius; Mars of Aries and Scorpio; Mercury of Gemini and Virgo. The moon was believed to rule Cancer, and the sun to rule Leo. In centuries to come, three more planets were discovered, so astrologers made Uranus the coruler of Aquarius; Neptune the coruler of Pisces; and Pluto the coruler of Scorpio.

In time, the study and practice of astrology spread from Babylon to Greece, Egypt, India — and later to Europe. At first astrologers cast horoscopes only for their countries and rulers, foretelling wars, plagues, famines, and conquests. Then the well-to-do began hiring their own personal astrologers to keep them clued in to the future. Johannes Kepler (1571-1630), the famous German astronomer, also had a full-time job as court astrologer to the Austrian emperor.

Out of the ancient belief in astrology grew the true science of astronomy. In fact, the foundations of astronomy were laid by those Babylonian priests who so carefully charted the movements of the planets and the positions of the stars which were visible to them. But as the science of astronomy grew more important, astrology grew less respectable. By the end of the 17th century, most scientists were labeling astrology as superstitious nonsense.

Oddly enough, in today's supersonic, science-minded world, astrology has suddenly gained a new popularity. Maybe the stars seem more friendly to us because we have less and less control over our lives. The complexities of automation also seem to drive many people to the occult for comfort. "Why use the I Ching and astrology in a world where you have supercomputers?" asks one student. "The answer is because you can't understand how the computers work — and even if you do, you have no control over them. Somehow, the occult makes more sense. It tells you that there are powers greater than the computers — powers you can use to control your life. You can't have that kind of relationship with a computer."

By now you've probably heard that we are "entering the Age of Aquarius." What does this mean?

According to astrologers, our sun moves backward along the zodiac; taking about 2,200 years to pass through each sign. These 2,200-

year passages are called *solar ages*. The Earth is already said to have passed through the Arian Age, the Taurean Age, and almost all the way through the Piscean Age. Some astrologers say that the Age of Aquarius will begin in 2200 A.D. Others seem to think that it has already begun.

When the sun passes through a sign, humanity is supposed to be influenced by the characteristics of that sign. For more than 2,100 years, the sun is supposed to have been in the constellation Pisces. Think about it. Have the last 2,100 years of history shown Piscean characteristics — an interest in spiritual and religious matters, exploration and commerce by sea, self-sacrifice, sorrow, illusion, oppression . . . ?

Astrologers think that the Aquarian Age will be a better time for everyone. They say it will be a time of joy, of scientific achievement, service to mankind, and great strides forward in the knowledge of our universe. "The minds of men will turn from earth and sea to contemplate the mysteries of the air," says astrologer Manly Hall. He points out that Aquarius rules humanitarians, explorers, psychologists, electricians, astronauts — and astrologers! It is more favorable for social work and international peace, unlike the Piscean Age, which astrologer Carroll Richter calls "an age of tears and sorrow, focused on the death of Christ."

The Age of Aquarius may not be all good, however. Aquarius is also the sign of change — and sometimes that means disruption just for the mere sake of change, turning everything upside down just to see how it looks that way. But if you have the sun in Aquarius (born Jan. 20 to Feb. 19), you don't need to be told that this is a sign of movers and shakers.

Casting a Horoscope

When an astrologer casts a horoscope, he divides the zodiac into a wheel-shape with 12 portions. Each portion is known as a "house," and each house is ruled by one of the 12 zodiac signs. Remember the clock face we told you to visualize when imagining the heavenly zodiac? Well, when an astrologer draws up your personal horoscope chart, he puts the first "house" (called "the House of Personality") at what would be nine o'clock; the second "house" (the way you use funds) at eight o'clock; the third "house" (relatives, mental ability) at seven o'clock; and so on. (The "Ascendant" or "Rising Sign" is placed on the "cusp" or dividing line between the 12th and 1st houses.)

Here is a rundown of the interests represented by the 12 houses in a horoscope chart:

First House: Personality, disposition, self-interest, the way you appear to others.

Second House: Financial affairs, gain or loss.

Third House: Relatives, short journeys, studies, mental ability.

Fourth House: Your family, early environment, conditions at beginning and end of life.

Fifth House: Children, pleasures, love affairs.

Sixth House: Health, servants or employees.

Seventh House: Partnerships (including mar-

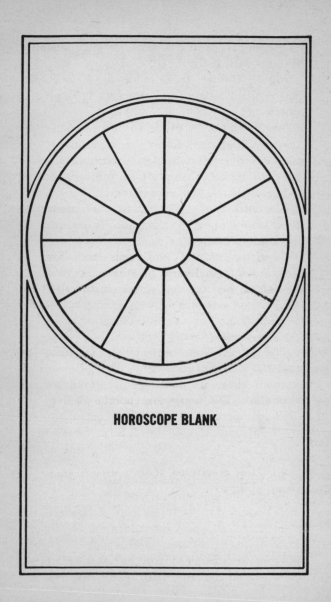

HOROSCOPE BLANK

riage), legal contracts and lawsuits, enemies, dealings with the public.

Eighth House: Inheritance, death and spiritual rebirth, money and property belonging to others.

Ninth House: Attitude toward religion, long journeys, higher education, your dreams, experiences in places far from your birthplace.

Tenth House: Your job or profession, fame and promotions, your employers.

Eleventh House: Your friends and associates, those who support you in your endeavors, your hopes and wishes.

Twelfth . House: Conditions which restrain or limit you (including hospitals and prisons), the hidden side of life, secrets (including secret sorrows and enemies), unexpected troubles, exile, seclusion.

The date of your birth determines what sign your sun is in, but in order to draw up your own personal chart, an astrologer must know your *ascendant*. The ascendant is the zodiac sign (and its degree) rising on the eastern horizon at the moment of your birth. Since there are 24 hours in a day, and 360 degrees in the zodiac (30 degrees in each sign), each degree will be on the eastern horizon four minutes. This means that although you and a friend may both be born on the same day — unless you are born at the same time and geographic location — you will probably have different ascendants, and quite different personalities, for the ascendant is always placed on the cusp (line dividing the houses of a horoscope) of the first house, the House of Personality.

Here's how it works. Let's say you were born on April 18th, with your sun in Aries. At the moment of your birth, however, the sign of Virgo was rising over the eastern horizon. Both Virgo and Aries will exert influence on you, for the sun represents your individuality, and the ascendant your personality. Arians are said to be active, positive, dominant, courageous, strong-willed, and independent. Virgoans are described as silent, receptive, loyal, fastidious, critical, and exacting. To get a picture of the real you, you must mix and blend the characteristics of the two signs.

Let's suppose Virgo is your ascendant. This means your second house is governed by Libra. (In any horoscope chart, the 12 signs of the zodiac always follow in the order shown on p. 8). Now, with careful Virgo in the first house, you might expect to be thrifty. But with Libra in the second house (the way you spend your money), you will have trouble balancing your checkbook. And with your sun in Aries in the eighth house, you may be too proud and independent to ask for what is rightfully yours.

As you can see, there's more to each individual horoscope than just saying, "I'm a Sagittarius," or "I'm a Gemini." Your sun sign represents the underlying foundation of your character, your *inner* self — but your ascendant governs the way that you appear and the way the world appears to you. It influences the way you look (especially the appearance of your face and head), your mannerisms and distinguishing characteristics, your attitudes and temperament.

Your Sun Sign and Your Inner Self

Your sun sign, or the sign you were born under, is the individual *you*, the inner self that others do not always see. It rules your will to be, your desire to achieve, your ambition to be something. The sun is the most powerful influence of all those lights in the sky, and the sign the sun was passing through at the moment of your birth stamps you with its characteristics. You may be a Gemini (sun) — Taurus (ascendant) — Scorpio (moon) person (or any other planetary combination), but astrologers say your Gemini sun characteristics will be the strongest factor in your horoscope. Now that you know this, you will want to zero in on more particular information about *your* sun sign. Here it is:

If you were born March 21 to April 20 —

YOUR SUN IS IN *ARIES*

Independence is your aim, and activity is your middle name. "What's happening?" and

"Where's the action?" are two of your favorite questions. You are constantly *doing*, here, there, and everywhere. You are fiery and impulsive, rushing bravely headfirst into every experience.

Your personality is forceful, dynamic, and self-assured. Fresh starts and new beginnings fascinate you. You're a born pioneer, daring to do what's never been done before. This love of adventure can lead you into places where other Sun signs fear to tread — but you would rather go it alone than be held up by those who aren't as quick on the draw. In fact, your character brims with bravery and daring, making you happiest when you're putting trailblazing plans into action.

Headfirst, like the Ram that symbolizes your sign, you seem to rush into every experience. You delight in doing things on the spur of the moment. Your convictions are strong and your courage is stirring. Your energy carries you full speed ahead. But all this Go power could result in rash and careless risk-taking. You tend to act first and ask questions later. Slow down and consider the consequences. Many rules and regulations are there for your protection. They aren't always repressive restrictions to rebel against. Soft-pedal your burning ambitions when you find them becoming too self-centered.

You want what you want when you want it — and that includes the time and attention of others. Yet you are often bored and impatient when you are asked to lend an ear to the trials and tribulations of another. Give something of yourself — it won't cost a bit of your precious independence. Tone down that quick temper and learn the fine art of tact. You needn't run over the other fellow to get where you're going. One word of praise for someone who needs it is worth a thousand patronizing putdowns. You can prove yourself, SuperRam, but try to do it without butting everyone else out of your way. Let that inner sympathy and sensitivity smooth your way.

You'll get along best with people born under the signs of Aquarius, Gemini, Leo, and Sagittarius. Red is the Arian color, and the ruby and bloodstone are the gems that express the Aries personality.

If you were born April 21 to May 20 —

YOUR SUN IS IN *TAURUS*

Practical, patient, persevering, and productive. These words describe you, trustworthy Taurus. But all that dependability doesn't make you dull because you are warmly emotional. Besides, your determined efforts often lead to success, although you take your time getting there. You're slow but sure, and you proceed with caution.

Money plays a big part in your plans. It's not that you're mercenary, but you know that financial success forms a secure foundation for life in this materialistic world. Anyway you do have a knack for tuning in to the true value of people and things.

Once you get your hands on money, you're far from miserly. You just like building up a bank balance because it makes you feel safe and secure. Besides, you have a healthy respect for the comforts that money can buy. You really appreciate the good things in life — good people, good times, and good food. In fact, your fondness for good food can lead to an unwelcome fund of fat. Don't be surprised if you have to diet most of your life, Taurus.

It takes a lot to make you mad, but those who know you will never bait you because they know you're liable to see red once your temper is aroused. That's when your bullish nature rears its frightening head! You make a terrible enemy, lowering your horns and digging in your heels. Pity the rash "bullfighter" who dares to take you and your fury on.

Luckily, your rages are few and far between. To your friends, you are usually kind and generous — and there's no one more romantic than Taurus when you're in love. But you are stubborn! You can be fixed in your opinions, and obstinate when challenged by the need for change. You like to hold onto things — whether they be people or prejudices. Learn to compromise. Life can't always conform to patterns that make you comfortable — and your opinion isn't the only one that's valid. Other people have rights and reasons, even if they don't always coincide with yours. Be firm — but don't be inflexible.

You'll get along best with people born under the signs of Scorpio, Cancer, Capricorn, Virgo, and Pisces. Blue and green are Taurus colors, and blue stones such as the sapphire, turquoise, and lapis-lazuli express the Taurus personality.

If you were born May 21 to June 21 —

YOUR SUN IS IN *GEMINI*

Snap, crackle, and pop! If your mental machinery could be heard, it might sound something like that, Gemini. Equipped with an amazing amount of mental energy, you're alert and agile in your quest for knowledge. You don't have to spend a lot of time hitting the books, for you seem to learn the most with the least effort. Many people regard you as a human storehouse of fascinating facts and figures. Actually, you gather a lot of information by asking questions, by mixing and matching observations, and by making the scene.

Oh, how you love to talk, talk, talk. And you speak so knowledgably on so many subjects that many of your listeners are impressed. But not everyone! There are those who see you as being superficial, a show-off with only a slick, surface intellect. Aren't they sometimes right? Wouldn't you rather skim the surface of things than ploddingly probe the depths?

Gemini is a double sign represented by a pair of heavenly Twins. That means that as a Gemini, you have a dual nature. You can think and do more than one thing at a time. Your mother may not believe it, but you are one of those rare creatures who can listen to the radio, talk on the telephone, and do your homework — all at once and without missing a beat. This can spell talent — or trouble. The trouble comes when you find it impossible to devote yourself to anything or anyone thoroughly and whole-heartedly. You're happy being here today and gone tomorrow. It's tough, but most of our dreams take time and toil to achieve. Develop a little patience and persistence.

Geminis should try to make "less talk and more action" their motto. Curb your impatience with those whose minds can't quite match yours. All that quick wit and fast talk can make you seem nervous, even jittery. Try to slow down a bit. Think before you speak, and then your glib tongue won't trip you up so often.

You'll get along best with people born under the signs of Leo, Aries, Aquarius, and Libra. Yellow is the Gemini color, and the agate is the gem the Romans claimed made the Gemini "come rejoicing home."

If you were born June 22 to July 22 —

YOUR SUN IS IN *CANCER*

In Latin, the word "cancer" means "crab," and a crab is what your nature resembles if you were born under this sign. Other people must exert time and effort to penetrate the protective shell with which you surround yourself. Shy and sensitive on the surface, you possess an inner core of strength and emotional depth.

You are sympathetic and unselfish. Even though you try to hide it, you are extremely emotional and dependent. Like the crab, you often sidestep situations and people because you are afraid of getting hurt. You may even present a defensively self-sufficient image to the world that says: "I'm all right. I can take care of myself!" But your eyes give you away. They say: "Take care of me. I need to be needed!"

Deep down you are full of fears and fantasies. Two of your biggest fears center around ridicule and rejection. That supersensitive nature of yours makes it hard for you to take the slightest bit of criticism. Sometimes you even imagine malice where none exists.

Conquer that inferiority complex now. Brush up on your self-confidence. Find a place to which you can withdraw and replenish your sense of security. Those born under Cancer often dream of the day when they can have a large, loving family of their own. This makes sense when you realize that Cancer is the "Tribal" sign of the zodiac, for Cancerians prize their ancestors and their heritage. A Cancerian can charm you with his ancestral coat of arms, and fascinate you with his family tree.

Home is definitely where your heart lies — but you may do a lot of wandering before you find the home you want to call your own. When that happens, you'll probably be able to afford to make it as comfortable as you want it. Although you are cautious and conservative when it comes to money, you know how to make a dollar double and even triple. Many millionaires are born under the sign of Cancer.

Learn to manage your moods. They are many-faced and multifaceted. Maintain a broad middleground between manic joy and melancholia.

There's nothing wrong with being emotional as long as you let your heart rule *with* your head.

You'll get along best with people born under the signs of Pisces, Scorpio, Taurus, and Virgo. White and silvery pastels are the colors that do the most for you, and the agate and moonstone are supposed to be your lucky gems.

If you were born July 23 to August 23 —

YOUR SUN IS IN *LEO*

Lordly Leo, the Lion-Hearted! "Let the Sunshine in" is your theme song. Your personality gives off a golden glow that warms even the coldest soul. You are chivalrous and noble. You turn away from anything that is dishonest, petty, or vulgar. Your standards are high, and so are your abilities.

Leos shine in the spotlight, for their favorite place is front and center. They thrive on attention and adulation. No second place for them, they want to be top cat on the totem pole. To get there, they don't mind using dramatic methods and colorful means.

You long to do great things in a grand manner, leading others along paths of glory. Your aristocratic dignity cries out for respect and recognition. But you are likely to withdraw with a princely pout whenever you feel that your talents are being ignored. Really, Leo, sometimes your intense pride is a royal pain!

Your generosity appears gallant — but aren't the motives behind it sometimes a little selfish? You give lavishly as long as those who receive what you offer reward you with their admiration and praise. Try helping others for the pure pleasure of helping, not for the gratitude or appreciation you think it will bring your way.

Bring your self-confidence down to size when you see it becoming arrogance. Don't boast, but let your deeds set shining and silent examples instead. Then you'll get the love and affection your radiant warmth deserves. But first you'll have to come off your pedestal, pussycat. Your demands on others, and your hunger for power could result in a revolution. And when your friends and family revolt, those pompous ways of yours could leave you out in the cold. Instead of blinding others with your sense of importance, share the brilliant light of your love and kindness with one and all. You'll be the greater for it.

You'll get along best with people born under the signs of Aries, Sagittarius, Libra, and Gemini. Gold and orange are your colors, the topaz and sardonyx your stones.

If you were born August 24 to September 23 —

YOUR SUN IS IN *VIRGO*

You set your sights high, Virgo. You try to be a paragon of purity in everything you think and do. But this love of purity doesn't mean that you are prim and prudish. Virgo is an Earth sign, first and foremost, and you are quite at home in this world. It's just that your desire for purity drives you to seek the plain, unvarnished truth. Your mind is sharp and chockful of common sense. Con men and counterfeiters leave you cold. You distrust anything which is phoney, pompous, or pretentious. You instinctively reserve your respect for the *real* thing.

You're a born analyst, Virgo. You delight in mentally dissecting people and problems to arrive at the essential truth of the matter. Your thought processes click along like a computer. First you collect the information or data you need. Then your mind chews up and digests every detail. After you have thoroughly examined all the tiny parts that make up the whole of your subject, you coolly come to a conclusion. No wonder the sign of Virgo is known as "the Critic" of the Zodiac.

The methods Virgo uses are painstaking and ultra-careful. This sometimes makes it difficult for you to maintain a proper perspective. Has anyone ever called you a "nit picker"? If so, it's because you became so devoted to details that you lost sight of the larger issues. You may often miss the forest for the trees. Remember, the forest *and* the individual trees make up the whole picture.

Your standards are high, and you have every right to demand the best of yourself. But this preoccupation with perfection can hinder your progress in an imperfect world. Bear in mind that people are complex and contradictory. They can't always meet your requirements. Narrow-minded disapproval and nagging are negative, and do more harm than good. "But I'm only trying to help!" you may cry in dismay. "I'm only telling you for your own good!" However, if your "trying to help" means carping and complaining, you'll find it does less good than your talent for cool, constructive comment.

Make the most of your talents, Virgo, especially those which make use of your fine, efficient mind. Perhaps you find it easy to express your quick wit in writing — many great writers are born under this sign. And when it comes to human relationships, offer kindness and compassion instead of mere criticism. Strengthen yourself by helping those who are weaker — Virgos find it natural to respond warmly to those in need. Service to something (or someone) outside yourself is the finest contribution you can make.

You'll get along best with people born under the signs of Capricorn, Taurus, Cancer, and Scorpio. Blue and gray are your colors. Gems such as carnelian, jasper, and chrysolite express the Virgo personality.

If you were born September 24 to October 23 —

YOUR SUN IS IN *LIBRA*

Peace on earth is more than just an ideal to you, Libra — but not peace at any price. You're a first-rate fighter for truth, justice, and equality although you rarely come to blows. Reason and rationality are the weapons you war with, and you have a good reputation as a referee or mediator. In fact, you often find yourself in the middle, mediating disputes and showdowns between people on both sides of the fence. This is because you try to tread the middle road of moderation, carefully weighing and measuring each and every side of an argument. Friends value your sense of justice. And you're a peacemaker par excellence because you seek solutions that are just and fair to all parties.

32

However, your private life is not always so peaceful. You may be great at balancing other people's books, but you have a terrible time making up your own mind. You teeter-totter, performing your balancing act (remember, Libra is the sign of the Scales). "If I do this, this will happen. But if I do that, that will happen. . . . All this choosing is confusing!" you think. The more alternatives, the more trouble you have in coming up with an answer. But don't lose your cool when confronted by a choice. Keep your calm and commit yourself to a course of action.

Pacifism is a beautiful policy, but if you go along with what you know to be wrong just to keep peace, the scales tip off balance, and you're the loser! Your gift for diplomacy becomes dangerous if it allows others to take advantage of you. To paraphrase Abraham Lincoln, "You can please some of the people some of the time. But you can't please all of the people all of the time." Keep the peace, but not at the price of your own principles.

Make your own decisions and carry them out. Your confidence will grow with the courage of your convictions. Don't fall for flattery, or endlessly angle for admiration. Know your own ideals and work to make them real. Only when you are at peace with the real you will your search for harmony lead to happiness instead of hang-ups.

You'll get along best with people born under the signs of Gemini, Aquarius, Leo, and Sagittarius. The colors your personality really vibrates to are rose and blue — including blue-green. If you're shopping for lucky gems, look for jade and rose quartz.

If you were born October 24 to November 22 —

YOUR SUN IS IN *SCORPIO*

You come on strong, Scorpio. Your intensity is as penetrating as a laser beam. Your energy is so abundant that it seems almost atomic, and your powers of concentration are formidable.

No one is more ambitious than you. You want the best life has to offer, and you want it on your own terms. But it's not the flashiness of fame that you seek, for you know that it's not always what's up front that counts. Being the power behind the throne suits you, for you prefer to maneuver from the background of any organization or enterprise.

They said it couldn't be done? Then they didn't know *you*! You thrive on challenges. Long after your competition has given up, your door-die brand of determination keeps you in there pitching.

"Still waters run deep" describes your temperament. Your complex, contradictory character keeps everyone guessing. You put up a carefully self-controlled front, but beneath this facade your emotions zig and zag from one extreme to the other. When you love or hate, it's with everything you've got, and you're not above seeking revenge when you think you've been wronged. By the same token, you're very protective of those you love — so much so that you can be too possessive and jealous.

Many people will feel that they never really know you. No wonder, when you keep those seething responses and reactions hidden beneath a supercool surface. Try lowering your guard and relaxing that reserve. How can others really appreciate you when you are so secretive about your motives, so subtle in your methods?

Sometimes, Scorpio, you are so relentless and ruthless that you sting friend and foe alike. Learn to forgive and forget. Now and then put yourself in the other fellow's place. Above all, don't let yourself be torn in two by doubts and suspicions about those you care for. Love requires trust if it is to grow.

Those born under Scorpio can usually see through the surface of illusion to the facts beneath. They're hard to fool, and that's why Scorpios often make good detectives and investigators. Whatever is secret and "undercover" intrigues you Scorpios — so much so that when you make one of your generous gestures, you probably do it secretly. That friend in need you aided may be still wondering who helped him out.

Scorpios get along best with people born under the signs of Cancer, Pisces, Virgo, and Capricorn. Gems with good vibes for them are the beryl, garnet, and sardonyx. Scorpio's colors are red and black.

If you were born November 23 to December 21 —

YOUR SUN IS IN *SAGITTARIUS*

The symbol of Sagittarius is a centaur, a mythological wonder, half-horse and half-man. This centaur is an archer, and his arrow is pointed toward the heavens. The direction of his aim, Sagittarius, tells you a lot about yourself. You're a straight-shooter, and you aim high, for the truth and for personal freedom. You are the rover and roamer of the zodiac. You can't bear to be cornered, cramped, or confined. Faraway places with strange-sounding names turn you on, and you're a seeker of wisdom on all your journeys. But sometimes your wanderlust carries you right off the deep end. Because you don't like to be tied down, you can be too quick to answer the call of the wild blue yonder.

Too much restlessness can make you seem unreliable, unable to handle responsibility. Putting things off is another one of your weak points. "I'll do it tomorrow," you say, but tomorrow never comes if you keep putting it off. Stop scattering your energies. An aimless archer never hits a target. Focus your forces on thoroughly completing the job at hand. Fulfill your promises and obligations. Responsibility need not mean restrictions. And your new found discipline will bring you freedom from frustration.

You're the eternal optimist, full of fun, good humor, and good cheer. Warm and outgoing, you have plenty of friends. You're too tolerant to have time for petty prejudices or narrow-mindedness. And there's no one more straightforward or sincere than Sagittarius. You say what you mean, and you mean what you say. But sometimes your freewheeling frankness finds you with your foot in your mouth. You mean well, but your blunt outspokenness often makes you appear rude or inconsiderate. The whole-truth-and-nothing-but approach can hurt as often as it helps. Try thinking before you speak. Train your tongue to be more tactful.

Sagittarians seem to be the luckiest of signs. Perhaps your luck stems from that sort of sixth sense you have for spotting winners. You can size up a situation, and then make it work *for* you because your intuition is almost always right on target. Combine that intuition with your intelligence and insight, and you've got a winning combination. You can afford to tune in to your instincts (they're on the side of what's fair and just), and to trust your hunches. Let your intuition be your inspiration and your guide.

You'll find compatible friends in those born under the signs of Aries, Leo, Libra, and Aquarius, and Capricorn. All shades of purple are harmonious to Sagittarius, and the amethyst is your gem.

If you were born December 22 to January 19 —

YOUR SUN IS IN *CAPRICORN*

"Life is real, life is earnest. . . ." These words might have been written just for you, Capricorn. You are as serious and single-minded in your upward climb as your zodiacal symbol, the mountain goat. Like you, these hardy goats don't mind clinging to mountainsides, enduring blinding blizzards and breathtaking gales. They know where they're going, so they have what it takes to get there.

What else have you got in common with Capricorn's symbol the mountain goat? Well, you're probably a solitary creature, often preferring your privacy to the company of others. And although you manage to pass all of Nature's tests and trials in your slow, steady climb to the mountain top, you're not foolhardy or reckless. Safety is uppermost with you, and you always look before you leap.

Once you set your sights on winning, nothing can stop you. Setbacks and obstacles only seem to make you more determined. You are willing to work harder and harder, and to do without all but bare necessities, if necessary. You know how to make one dollar do the work of two or three — in fact, if you don't watch out, you could become downright stingy and miserly.

It takes time and effort to know what makes a Capricorn tick. On the surface, they are often dignified, conservative, and aloof. But behind that lone-wolf image there lurks a longing for warmth and friendly contact. Come on, Capricorn! Loosen up and learn to laugh at yourself. Don't be so self-conscious. Socialize and be spontaneous. "Easier said than done," you may grumble, but would it help you to know that the older most Capricorns get, the less uptight they become?

Capricorns are ultra-conscientious. They tend to forget that all work and no play can make anyone dull and miserable. They should try for a little R and R (Armyese for "rest and recreation"). And they should also try not to take on more work than they can handle, because their consciences will torment them if they find they can't fulfill an obligation.

You tend to be the workhorse and worrywart of the zodiac, Capricorn. You can reach the depths of depression by worrying and wondering why it's taking you so long to reach your goal — but pessimism will only slow you down. So think positive and have faith. All things come to those who serve and wait, Capricorn. Heed these words if you not only want to climb mountains, but to move them.

You'll find good companions and friends among those born under the signs of Virgo, Taurus, Pisces, and Scorpio. Dark blues and browns are your colors, and amber and smoky quartz are your gems.

If you were born January 20 to February 19 —

YOUR SUN IS IN *AQUARIUS*

Your "age" is said to be just around the corner, Aquarius, but you're already far ahead of the world when it comes to ideas and ideals. You never follow the crowd — not if you can find a way to lead it. Your mind is inspired and inventive, and you're no slouch at dreaming that so-called "impossible dream." As far as Aquarius is concerned, nothing is impossible.

You're very creative in everything you do. And you are a Do-er! Once involved with work you care about, you are likely to forget about everything else. So choose your life work carefully, for you will spend much of your energy and time on it. Whatever you decide to do, try to avoid dull, routine, dead-end jobs — they will only drive you up the wall. And if you become the boss, don't be surprised if your employees think you're a tough one. You'll expect everyone to work just as hard and carefully as you do.

"Liberty for all!" might be an Aquarian slogan. You not only demand freedom for yourself, but for everyone else. Some may consider you a rebel, but you only rebel at things you think are unjust and unfair. You appreciate traditions as much as anyone, as long as they are traditions that represent ability and achievement. But once a belief or tradition gets in the way of progress, you're ready to discard it.

Do others think you're hard to know? Stand-offish? Aloof? The truth is, you're somewhat shy. It's hard for you to be open and outgoing until you know how the other person feels. But once you make a friend, it's for keeps. Aquarians are loyal and generous to those they care about.

But even with friends, you don't like to be pinned down. Maybe that's why you're so often late for dates and appointments. Of course no one stays angry at you for long (you're such a whiz at apologies), but is it really fair to waste the time of others this way?

It has been said that more than three fourths of the names enshrined in the Hall of Fame belong to Aquarians, which certainly shows that Aquarians are achievers. But the true Aquarian doesn't set out to achieve just for his own glory. He really wants to somehow benefit society, to leave the Earth a little better than he found it. Humanity turns him on — with certain exceptions, that is. Bigots of all kinds and ego-trippers leave him cold. And if you're an Aquarian, keep that word "cold" always in mind. You may often seem too detached and impersonal to others. The truth is, you're so determined to solve the problems of the world's millions that you have a hard time relating to individual humans who want a little of your time.

You'll get along best with other Aquarians, but you also find Geminis and Librans very compatible. Sagittarians bring out the best in you. Your colors are off-beat shades of red, blue, and green. The sapphire is your stone.

If you were born February 19 to March 21 —

YOUR SUN IS IN *PISCES*

Remember that old song called "Beautiful Dreamer"? It was probably written about a Piscean. Imaginative, intuitive, romantic — you Pisces-born often prefer to live a life of the mind. But no one should write you off as just daydreamers. Pisces is symbolized by two fishes, linked, yet swimming their separate ways. That means there are two sides to the Pisces nature — the dreamer and the worker who turns those dreams into reality. Think of George Washington, Albert Einstein, and Mike Mansfield — they represent the Piscean nature in its highest form.

If you were born under the sign of Pisces, you probably wonder why others seem to always be telling you their troubles and secrets. The answer is because you're so sympathetic and discreet. (Pisceans know how to button their lips.) You have the ability to put yourself in the other fellow's place, and know just how he feels. In fact, you're so sensitive to the wavelengths of your friends that you seem to know when they're troubled and upset — even when they say nothing. It is almost as though your mind vibrates like a tuning fork to the feelings of others.

In spite of this sensitivity and warmth, Pisceans worry a lot about being rejected. They shouldn't, for it is easy to be fond of them because of their kindness and sympathy. A true Piscean puts others first, sometimes to the point of becoming a doormat for those who take advantage of him. Then, likely as not, he picks himself up and goes off to nurse his hurt feelings. Brooding and self-pity can be big Piscean faults. If that's your problem, here's a remedy: Stop letting yourself be pushed around. Others won't take advantage of you unless you invite them to. The next time a friend asks you to take over his chores or homework, remember you need the time to do your own. Sympathize with him, but make him stand on his own feet instead of yours. It's better for both of you.

If you're a Pisces, you probably have a trick memory. You store away facts and impressions, and then bring them out when you need them. This can help you do well in school — if you don't spend too much time daydreaming. Your mind seems to pick out and absorb the important points in a lesson without too much study. But it's probable that your brain doesn't always work as well with dates and figures — which could give you trouble when it comes to history or math.

But whenever there's creative work to be done, Pisceans can be found. Artistic, imaginative, intuitive — no wonder there are so many Piscean writers, artists, and designers. And because they are so sympathetic and like to care for others, they make good nurses and doctors. Pisceans are also among our finest actresses and actors because they absorb impressions so easily.

Money, however, is not a Piscean trip. You make it, then you probably spend it on impulse or give it away. All too often Pisceans are known as "easy touches," turning out their pockets at any hard-luck story. Then when your bank balance dwindles, you worry and fret. You need the security that funds can provide, so learn to

44

save systematically and spend more carefully.

Even more than money, Pisces, you probably need peace and quiet. Get off by yourself often to relax and think things out. Try to avoid quarrelsome people and disturbing situations. This also refers to messy surroundings. If your room looks like a hurricane just whizzed through, straighten it up. Disorder on the outside can make you feel chaotic on the inside.

Pisceans get along best with those born under the signs of Cancer, Scorpio, Taurus, and Capricorn. Your colors are green and greenish blues. Quartz, opal, and green beryl are your gems.

Finding Your Moon

You know where your Sun sign is, but how about your Moon? Whatever sign the moon was passing through on the day of your birth has, according to astrologers, a lot to do with your personality and your feelings. We all know that the moon influences the ebb and flow of the tides. Astrologers say that it also influences the ebb and flow of your moods, the ups and downs of your disposition.

Whether or not this is true, it is fairly easy to find just where the moon was, zodiac-wise, at the time of your birth. Look at the following tables. Find the one headed by the year of your birth. Then notice the little zodiac sign beside the month and day nearest your birthday (see zodiac symbols below).

Notice that the moon changes position about every two days. So, if you were born on the fourth of January in 1952, for example, your moon would be in Aries. On the fifth of January in that year, the moon moved into Taurus.

Here are the zodiac signs and their symbols:

♈ ARIES	♉ TAURUS	♊ GEMINI
♋ CANCER	♌ LEO	♍ VIRGO
♎ LIBRA	♏ SCORPIO	♐ SAGITTARIUS
♑ CAPRICORN	♒ AQUARIUS	♓ PISCES

Now turn to the tables on the next few pages and locate your Moon sign. On the pages following the tables, check out what the location of your Moon means to you.

1950

JAN.	FEB.	MAR.	APR.	MAY	JUNE	JULY	AUG.	SEPT.	OCT.	NOV.	DEC.
3 ♋	1 ♌	1 ♌	2 ♎	1 ♏	1 ♑	1 ♒	2 ♈	1 ♉	3 ♋	2 ♌	1 ♍
5 ♌	4 ♍	3 ♍	4 ♏	3 ♐	3 ♒	3 ♓	4 ♉	3 ♊	5 ♌	4 ♍	4 ♎
7 ♍	6 ♎	5 ♎	6 ♐	5 ♑	6 ♓	5 ♈	7 ♊	6 ♋	8 ♍	6 ♎	6 ♏
9 ♎	8 ♏	7 ♏	8 ♑	7 ♒	8 ♈	8 ♉	9 ♋	8 ♌	10 ♎	8 ♏	8 ♐
12 ♏	10 ♐	9 ♐	10 ♒	9 ♓	11 ♉	10 ♊	12 ♌	10 ♍	12 ♏	10 ♐	10 ♑
14 ♐	12 ♑	11 ♑	12 ♓	12 ♈	13 ♊	13 ♋	14 ♍	12 ♎	14 ♐	12 ♑	12 ♒
16 ♑	14 ♒	14 ♒	15 ♈	14 ♉	16 ♋	15 ♌	16 ♎	14 ♏	16 ♑	14 ♒	14 ♓
18 ♒	17 ♓	16 ♓	17 ♉	17 ♊	18 ♌	18 ♍	18 ♏	17 ♐	18 ♒	17 ♓	16 ♈
20 ♓	19 ♈	18 ♈	20 ♊	19 ♋	20 ♍	20 ♎	20 ♐	19 ♑	20 ♓	19 ♈	19 ♉
23 ♈	22 ♉	21 ♉	22 ♋	22 ♌	22 ♎	22 ♏	22 ♑	21 ♒	23 ♈	21 ♉	21 ♊
25 ♉	24 ♊	23 ♊	25 ♌	24 ♍	25 ♏	24 ♐	25 ♒	23 ♓	25 ♉	24 ♊	24 ♋
28 ♊	27 ♋	26 ♋	27 ♍	26 ♎	27 ♐	26 ♑	27 ♓	25 ♈	28 ♊	27 ♋	26 ♌
30 ♋		28 ♌	29 ♎	28 ♏	29 ♑	28 ♒	29 ♈	28 ♉	30 ♋	29 ♌	29 ♍
		30 ♍		30 ♐		30 ♓		30 ♊			31 ♎

1951

JAN.	FEB.	MAR.	APR.	MAY	JUNE	JULY	AUG.	SEPT.	OCT.	NOV.	DEC.
2 ♏	1 ♐	2 ♑	2 ♓	2 ♈	1 ♉	3 ♋	2 ♍	3 ♎	2 ♏	1 ♐	2 ♒
4 ♐	3 ♑	4 ♒	5 ♈	4 ♉	3 ♊	5 ♌	4 ♎	5 ♏	4 ♐	3 ♑	4 ♓
6 ♑	5 ♒	6 ♓	7 ♉	7 ♊	6 ♋	8 ♍	6 ♏	7 ♐	7 ♑	5 ♒	6 ♈
8 ♒	7 ♓	8 ♈	10 ♊	9 ♋	8 ♌	10 ♎	9 ♐	9 ♑	9 ♒	7 ♓	9 ♉
10 ♓	9 ♈	11 ♉	12 ♋	12 ♌	10 ♍	13 ♏	11 ♑	11 ♒	11 ♓	9 ♈	11 ♊
13 ♈	11 ♉	13 ♊	15 ♌	14 ♍	13 ♎	15 ♐	13 ♒	13 ♓	13 ♈	12 ♉	14 ♋
15 ♉	14 ♊	16 ♋	17 ♍	17 ♎	15 ♏	17 ♑	15 ♓	15 ♈	15 ♉	14 ♊	16 ♌
18 ♊	16 ♋	18 ♌	19 ♎	19 ♏	17 ♐	19 ♒	18 ♈	18 ♉	18 ♊	16 ♋	19 ♍
20 ♋	18 ♌	21 ♍	21 ♏	21 ♐	19 ♑	21 ♓	20 ♉	20 ♊	20 ♋	19 ♌	21 ♎
23 ♌	21 ♍	23 ♎	23 ♐	23 ♑	21 ♒	23 ♈	23 ♊	23 ♋	23 ♌	21 ♍	23 ♏
25 ♍	23 ♎	25 ♏	25 ♑	25 ♒	23 ♓	25 ♉	25 ♋	25 ♌	25 ♍	24 ♎	26 ♐
27 ♎	26 ♏	27 ♐	27 ♒	27 ♓	25 ♈	28 ♊	28 ♌	28 ♍	27 ♎	26 ♏	28 ♑
29 ♏	28 ♐	29 ♑	30 ♓	29 ♈	28 ♉	30 ♋	30 ♍	30 ♎	30 ♏	28 ♐	30 ♒
		31 ♒			30 ♊					30 ♑	

1952

JAN.	FEB.	MAR.	APR.	MAY	JUNE	JULY	AUG.	SEPT.	OCT.	NOV.	DEC.
1 ♓	1 ♉	2 ♊	1 ♋	1 ♌	2 ♎	2 ♏	2 ♑	1 ♒	2 ♈	1 ♉	3 ♋
3 ♈	4 ♊	5 ♋	3 ♌	3 ♍	4 ♏	4 ♐	4 ♒	3 ♓	4 ♉	3 ♊	5 ♌
5 ♉	6 ♋	7 ♌	6 ♍	6 ♎	7 ♐	6 ♑	6 ♓	5 ♈	7 ♊	5 ♋	8 ♍
7 ♊	9 ♌	10 ♍	8 ♎	8 ♏	9 ♑	8 ♒	8 ♈	7 ♉	9 ♋	8 ♌	10 ♎
10 ♋	11 ♍	12 ♎	11 ♏	10 ♐	11 ♒	10 ♓	11 ♉	10 ♊	11 ♌	10 ♍	13 ♏
12 ♌	14 ♎	14 ♏	13 ♐	12 ♑	13 ♓	12 ♈	13 ♊	12 ♋	14 ♍	13 ♎	15 ♐
15 ♍	16 ♏	17 ♐	15 ♑	14 ♒	15 ♈	14 ♉	15 ♋	15 ♌	16 ♎	15 ♏	17 ♑
17 ♎	18 ♐	19 ♑	17 ♒	16 ♓	17 ♉	17 ♊	18 ♌	17 ♍	19 ♏	17 ♐	19 ♒
20 ♏	20 ♑	21 ♒	19 ♓	19 ♈	19 ♊	19 ♋	20 ♍	19 ♎	21 ♐	20 ♑	21 ♓
22 ♐	22 ♒	23 ♓	21 ♈	21 ♉	22 ♋	22 ♌	22 ♎	21 ♏	24 ♑	22 ♒	23 ♈
24 ♑	24 ♓	25 ♈	24 ♉	23 ♊	24 ♌	24 ♍	25 ♏	24 ♐	26 ♒	24 ♓	26 ♉
26 ♒	27 ♈	27 ♉	26 ♊	26 ♋	27 ♍	27 ♎	28 ♐	26 ♑	28 ♓	26 ♈	28 ♊
28 ♓	29 ♉	29 ♊	28 ♋	28 ♌	29 ♎	29 ♏	30 ♑	28 ♒	30 ♈	28 ♉	30 ♋
30 ♈				31 ♍		31 ♐		30 ♓		30 ♊	

1953

JAN.	FEB.	MAR.	APR.	MAY	JUNE	JULY	AUG.	SEPT.	OCT.	NOV.	DEC.
1 ♌	3 ♎	2 ♎	1 ♏	3 ♑	1 ♒	1 ♓	1 ♉	2 ♋	1 ♌	3 ♎	2 ♏
4 ♍	5 ♏	4 ♏	3 ♐	5 ♒	3 ♓	3 ♈	3 ♊	4 ♌	4 ♍	5 ♏	5 ♐
6 ♎	8 ♐	7 ♐	5 ♑	7 ♓	5 ♈	5 ♉	5 ♋	7 ♍	6 ♎	8 ♐	7 ♑
9 ♏	10 ♑	9 ♑	8 ♒	9 ♈	7 ♉	8 ♊	7 ♌	9 ♎	9 ♏	10 ♑	9 ♒
11 ♐	12 ♒	11 ♒	10 ♓	11 ♉	10 ♊	10 ♋	9 ♍	12 ♏	11 ♐	12 ♒	12 ♓
13 ♑	14 ♓	13 ♓	12 ♈	13 ♊	12 ♋	12 ♌	13 ♎	14 ♐	14 ♑	14 ♓	14 ♈
15 ♒	16 ♈	15 ♈	14 ♉	15 ♋	14 ♌	14 ♍	15 ♏	16 ♑	16 ♒	17 ♈	16 ♉
17 ♓	18 ♉	17 ♉	16 ♊	17 ♌	16 ♍	17 ♎	16 ♐	18 ♒	18 ♓	19 ♉	18 ♊
19 ♈	20 ♊	19 ♊	18 ♋	20 ♍	19 ♎	19 ♏	20 ♑	21 ♓	20 ♈	21 ♊	20 ♋
22 ♉	22 ♋	22 ♋	20 ♌	23 ♎	22 ♏	21 ♐	22 ♒	23 ♈	22 ♉	23 ♋	22 ♌
24 ♊	25 ♌	24 ♌	23 ♍	25 ♏	24 ♐	24 ♑	24 ♓	25 ♉	24 ♊	25 ♌	25 ♍
26 ♋	27 ♍	27 ♍	26 ♎	28 ♐	26 ♑	26 ♒	26 ♈	27 ♊	26 ♋	27 ♍	27 ♎
29 ♌		29 ♎	28 ♏	30 ♑	28 ♒	28 ♓	28 ♉	29 ♋	29 ♌	30 ♎	30 ♏
31 ♍			30 ♐			30 ♈	30 ♊		31 ♍		

JAN.	FEB.	MAR.	APR.	MAY	JUNE	JULY	AUG.	SEPT.	OCT.	NOV.	DEC.
1 ♐	2 ♒	2 ♒	2 ♈	2 ♉	2 ♋	2 ♌	3 ♎	1 ♏	1 ♐	2 ♒	2 ♓
4 ♑	4 ♓	4 ♓	4 ♉	4 ♊	4 ♌	4 ♍	5 ♏	4 ♐	4 ♑	5 ♓	4 ♈
6 ♒	6 ♈	6 ♈	6 ♊	6 ♋	6 ♍	6 ♎	8 ♐	6 ♑	6 ♒	7 ♈	6 ♉
8 ♓	8 ♉	8 ♉	8 ♋	8 ♌	9 ♎	9 ♏	10 ♑	9 ♒	8 ♓	9 ♉	8 ♊
10 ♈	11 ♊	10 ♊	11 ♌	10 ♍	12 ♏	11 ♐	12 ♒	11 ♓	11 ♈	11 ♊	10 ♋
12 ♉	13 ♋	12 ♋	13 ♍	13 ♎	14 ♐	14 ♑	15 ♓	13 ♈	13 ♉	13 ♋	12 ♌
14 ♊	15 ♌	14 ♌	15 ♎	16 ♏	16 ♑	16 ♒	17 ♈	15 ♉	15 ♊	15 ♌	15 ♍
16 ♋	17 ♍	17 ♍	18 ♏	18 ♐	19 ♒	18 ♓	19 ♉	17 ♊	17 ♋	17 ♍	17 ♎
19 ♌	19 ♎	19 ♎	20 ♐	20 ♑	21 ♓	21 ♈	21 ♊	19 ♋	19 ♌	20 ♎	20 ♏
21 ♍	22 ♏	22 ♏	23 ♑	23 ♒	23 ♈	23 ♉	23 ♋	22 ♌	21 ♍	22 ♏	22 ♐
24 ♎	25 ♐	24 ♐	25 ♒	25 ♓	25 ♉	25 ♊	25 ♌	24 ♍	24 ♎	25 ♐	25 ♑
26 ♏	27 ♑	27 ♑	28 ♓	27 ♈	27 ♊	27 ♋	28 ♍	26 ♎	26 ♏	27 ♑	27 ♒
29 ♐		29 ♒	30 ♈	29 ♉	29 ♋	29 ♌	30 ♎	29 ♏	29 ♐	30 ♒	29 ♓
31 ♑		31 ♓		31 ♊		31 ♍			31 ♑		

JAN.	FEB.	MAR.	APR.	MAY	JUNE	JULY	AUG.	SEPT.	OCT.	NOV.	DEC.
1 ♈	1 ♊	2 ♋	1 ♌	3 ♎	1 ♏	1 ♐	2 ♒	1 ♓	1 ♈	1 ♊	1 ♋
3 ♉	3 ♋	5 ♌	3 ♍	5 ♏	4 ♐	4 ♑	5 ♓	3 ♈	3 ♉	3 ♋	3 ♌
5 ♊	5 ♌	7 ♍	5 ♎	8 ♐	6 ♑	6 ♒	7 ♈	6 ♉	5 ♊	5 ♌	5 ♍
7 ♋	7 ♍	9 ♎	8 ♏	10 ♑	9 ♒	9 ♓	9 ♉	8 ♊	7 ♋	8 ♍	7 ♎
9 ♌	10 ♎	12 ♏	10 ♐	13 ♒	11 ♓	11 ♈	11 ♊	10 ♋	9 ♌	10 ♎	10 ♏
11 ♍	12 ♏	14 ♐	13 ♑	15 ♓	14 ♈	13 ♉	14 ♋	12 ♌	11 ♍	12 ♏	12 ♐
13 ♎	14 ♐	17 ♑	15 ♒	19 ♈	16 ♉	15 ♊	16 ♌	14 ♍	14 ♎	15 ♐	15 ♑
16 ♏	17 ♑	19 ♒	18 ♓	21 ♉	18 ♊	17 ♋	18 ♍	16 ♎	16 ♏	17 ♑	17 ♒
18 ♐	19 ♒	21 ♓	20 ♈	23 ♊	20 ♋	19 ♌	20 ♎	19 ♏	18 ♐	20 ♒	20 ♓
21 ♑	22 ♓	23 ♈	22 ♉	25 ♋	22 ♌	21 ♍	22 ♏	21 ♐	21 ♑	22 ♓	22 ♈
23 ♒	24 ♈	26 ♉	24 ♊	28 ♌	24 ♍	24 ♎	25 ♐	24 ♑	23 ♒	25 ♈	24 ♉
26 ♓	26 ♉	28 ♊	26 ♋	30 ♍	26 ♎	26 ♏	27 ♑	26 ♒	26 ♓	27 ♉	26 ♊
28 ♈	28 ♊	30 ♋	28 ♌		29 ♏	28 ♐	29 ♒	28 ♈	28 ♈	29 ♊	28 ♋
30 ♉			30 ♍			31 ♑			30 ♉		30 ♌

JAN.	FEB.	MAR.	APR.	MAY	JUNE	JULY	AUG.	SEPT.	OCT.	NOV.	DEC.
1 ♍	2 ♏	3 ♐	2 ♑	2 ♒	3 ♈	2 ♉	1 ♊	1 ♌	1 ♍	1 ♏	1 ♐
3 ♎	5 ♐	5 ♑	4 ♒	4 ♓	5 ♉	5 ♊	3 ♋	3 ♍	3 ♎	4 ♐	3 ♑
6 ♏	7 ♑	8 ♒	7 ♓	6 ♈	7 ♊	7 ♋	5 ♌	6 ♎	5 ♏	6 ♑	6 ♒
8 ♐	10 ♒	10 ♓	9 ♈	9 ♉	9 ♋	9 ♌	7 ♍	8 ♏	7 ♐	9 ♒	8 ♓
11 ♑	12 ♓	13 ♈	11 ♉	11 ♊	11 ♌	11 ♍	9 ♎	10 ♐	9 ♑	11 ♓	11 ♈
13 ♒	14 ♈	15 ♉	13 ♊	13 ♋	13 ♍	13 ♎	11 ♏	12 ♑	12 ♒	14 ♈	13 ♉
16 ♓	17 ♉	17 ♊	16 ♋	15 ♌	15 ♎	15 ♏	14 ♐	15 ♒	14 ♓	16 ♉	16 ♊
18 ♈	19 ♊	19 ♋	18 ♌	17 ♍	18 ♏	17 ♐	16 ♑	17 ♓	17 ♈	18 ♊	18 ♋
20 ♉	21 ♋	21 ♌	20 ♍	19 ♎	20 ♐	20 ♑	19 ♒	20 ♈	19 ♉	20 ♋	20 ♌
23 ♊	23 ♌	23 ♍	22 ♎	21 ♏	23 ♑	22 ♒	21 ♓	22 ♉	22 ♊	22 ♌	22 ♍
25 ♋	25 ♍	26 ♎	24 ♏	24 ♐	25 ♒	25 ♓	24 ♈	24 ♋	24 ♍	24 ♍	24 ♎
27 ♌	27 ♎	28 ♏	27 ♐	26 ♑	28 ♓	27 ♈	26 ♉	27 ♋	26 ♌	27 ♎	26 ♏
29 ♍	29 ♏	30 ♐	29 ♑	29 ♒	30 ♈	30 ♉	28 ♊	29 ♌	28 ♍	29 ♏	28 ♐
31 ♎				31 ♓			30 ♋		30 ♎		31 ♑

JAN.	FEB.	MAR.	APR.	MAY	JUNE	JULY	AUG.	SEPT.	OCT.	NOV.	DEC.
2 ♒	1 ♓	3 ♈	1 ♉	1 ♊	2 ♌	1 ♍	2 ♏	2 ♑	2 ♒	1 ♓	1 ♈
5 ♓	4 ♈	5 ♉	4 ♊	3 ♋	4 ♍	3 ♎	4 ♐	5 ♒	5 ♓	3 ♈	3 ♉
7 ♈	6 ♉	8 ♊	6 ♋	5 ♌	6 ♎	5 ♏	6 ♑	7 ♓	7 ♈	6 ♉	6 ♊
10 ♉	8 ♊	10 ♋	8 ♍	8 ♍	8 ♏	8 ♐	9 ♒	10 ♈	10 ♉	8 ♊	8 ♋
12 ♊	10 ♋	12 ♌	10 ♍	10 ♎	10 ♐	10 ♑	11 ♓	12 ♉	12 ♊	11 ♋	10 ♌
14 ♋	12 ♌	14 ♍	12 ♎	12 ♏	13 ♑	12 ♒	14 ♈	15 ♊	14 ♋	13 ♌	12 ♍
16 ♌	14 ♍	16 ♎	14 ♏	14 ♐	15 ♒	15 ♓	16 ♉	17 ♋	17 ♌	15 ♍	14 ♎
18 ♍	16 ♎	18 ♏	17 ♐	16 ♑	18 ♓	17 ♈	19 ♊	19 ♌	19 ♍	17 ♎	16 ♏
20 ♎	19 ♏	20 ♐	19 ♑	19 ♒	20 ♈	20 ♉	21 ♋	21 ♍	21 ♎	19 ♏	19 ♐
22 ♏	21 ♐	23 ♑	21 ♒	22 ♓	22 ♉	22 ♊	23 ♌	23 ♍	23 ♏	21 ♐	21 ♑
25 ♐	23 ♑	25 ♒	24 ♓	24 ♈	24 ♊	24 ♋	25 ♍	25 ♎	25 ♐	23 ♑	23 ♒
27 ♑	26 ♒	28 ♓	26 ♈	26 ♉	25 ♋	26 ♌	27 ♎	27 ♐	27 ♑	26 ♒	26 ♓
29 ♒	28 ♓	30 ♈	29 ♉	28 ♊	28 ♍	28 ♍	29 ♏	30 ♑	29 ♒	28 ♓	28 ♈
				31 ♋	30 ♎	31 ♐	31 ♐				31 ♉

1958

JAN.	FEB.	MAR.	APR.	MAY	JUNE	JULY	AUG.	SEPT.	OCT.	NOV.	DEC.
2 ♊	1 ♋	2 ♌	1 ♍	2 ♏	1 ♐	2 ♒	1 ♓	2 ♉	2 ♊	1 ♋	3 ♍
4 ♋	3 ♌	4 ♍	3 ♎	4 ♐	3 ♑	5 ♓	3 ♈	5 ♊	5 ♋	3 ♌	5 ♎
6 ♌	5 ♍	6 ♎	5 ♏	6 ♑	5 ♒	7 ♈	6 ♉	7 ♋	7 ♌	5 ♍	7 ♏
8 ♍	7 ♎	8 ♏	7 ♐	8 ♒	7 ♓	10 ♉	9 ♊	10 ♌	9 ♍	7 ♎	9 ♐
11 ♎	9 ♏	10 ♐	9 ♑	11 ♓	10 ♈	12 ♊	11 ♋	12 ♍	11 ♎	9 ♏	11 ♑
13 ♏	11 ♐	13 ♑	11 ♒	14 ♈	12 ♉	15 ♋	13 ♌	14 ♎	13 ♏	12 ♐	13 ♒
15 ♐	13 ♑	15 ♒	14 ♓	16 ♉	15 ♊	17 ♌	15 ♍	16 ♏	15 ♐	14 ♑	15 ♓
17 ♑	16 ♒	17 ♓	16 ♈	18 ♊	17 ♋	19 ♍	17 ♎	18 ♐	17 ♑	16 ♒	18 ♈
19 ♒	18 ♓	20 ♈	19 ♉	21 ♋	19 ♌	21 ♎	19 ♏	20 ♑	19 ♒	18 ♓	20 ♉
22 ♓	21 ♈	23 ♉	21 ♊	23 ♌	22 ♍	23 ♏	21 ♐	22 ♒	22 ♓	21 ♈	23 ♊
24 ♈	23 ♉	25 ♊	24 ♋	25 ♍	24 ♎	25 ♐	24 ♑	25 ♓	24 ♈	23 ♉	25 ♋
27 ♉	26 ♊	27 ♋	26 ♌	28 ♎	26 ♏	27 ♑	26 ♒	27 ♈	27 ♉	26 ♊	28 ♌
29 ♊	28 ♋	30 ♌	28 ♍	30 ♏	28 ♐	30 ♒	28 ♓	30 ♉	29 ♊	28 ♋	30 ♍
			30 ♎		30 ♑	31 ♈	31 ♈			30 ♌	

1959

JAN.	FEB.	MAR.	APR.	MAY	JUNE	JULY	AUG.	SEPT.	OCT.	NOV.	DEC.
1 ♎	2 ♐	1 ♐	1 ♒	1 ♓	2 ♉	2 ♊	1 ♋	2 ♍	1 ♎	2 ♐	1 ♑
3 ♏	4 ♑	3 ♑	4 ♓	3 ♈	5 ♊	5 ♋	3 ♌	4 ♎	3 ♏	4 ♑	3 ♒
5 ♐	6 ♒	5 ♒	6 ♈	6 ♉	8 ♋	7 ♌	6 ♍	6 ♏	6 ♐	6 ♒	6 ♓
7 ♑	8 ♓	7 ♓	9 ♉	8 ♊	10 ♌	9 ♍	8 ♎	8 ♐	8 ♑	8 ♓	8 ♈
10 ♒	11 ♈	10 ♈	11 ♊	11 ♋	12 ♍	12 ♎	10 ♏	10 ♑	10 ♒	11 ♈	11 ♉
12 ♓	13 ♉	12 ♉	14 ♋	13 ♌	14 ♎	14 ♏	12 ♐	13 ♒	12 ♓	13 ♉	13 ♊
14 ♈	16 ♊	15 ♊	16 ♌	16 ♍	16 ♏	16 ♐	14 ♑	15 ♓	14 ♈	16 ♊	15 ♋
17 ♉	18 ♋	17 ♋	18 ♍	18 ♎	18 ♐	18 ♑	16 ♒	17 ♈	17 ♉	18 ♋	18 ♌
19 ♊	20 ♌	19 ♌	21 ♎	20 ♏	20 ♑	20 ♒	18 ♓	19 ♉	19 ♊	21 ♌	20 ♍
22 ♋	23 ♍	22 ♍	23 ♏	22 ♐	22 ♒	22 ♓	21 ♈	22 ♊	22 ♋	23 ♍	23 ♎
24 ♌	25 ♎	24 ♎	25 ♐	24 ♑	25 ♓	24 ♈	23 ♉	24 ♋	24 ♌	25 ♎	25 ♏
26 ♍	27 ♏	26 ♏	27 ♑	26 ♒	27 ♈	27 ♉	26 ♊	27 ♌	27 ♍	27 ♏	27 ♐
28 ♎	.	28 ♐	29 ♒	28 ♓	29 ♉	29 ♊	28 ♋	29 ♍	29 ♎	29 ♐	29 ♑
31 ♏		30 ♑		31 ♈		31 ♋	31 ♌		31 ♏		31 ♒

1960

JAN.	FEB.	MAR.	APR.	MAY	JUNE	JULY	AUG.	SEPT.	OCT.	NOV.	DEC.
2 ♓	1 ♈	1 ♉	3 ♋	2 ♌	1 ♍	1 ♎	2 ♐	2 ♒	1 ♓	2 ♉	2 ♊
4 ♈	3 ♉	4 ♊	5 ♌	5 ♍	4 ♎	3 ♏	4 ♑	4 ♓	4 ♈	4 ♊	4 ♋
7 ♉	5 ♊	6 ♋	8 ♍	7 ♎	6 ♏	5 ♐	6 ♒	6 ♈	6 ♉	7 ♋	7 ♌
9 ♊	8 ♋	9 ♌	10 ♎	9 ♏	8 ♐	7 ♑	8 ♓	8 ♉	8 ♊	9 ♌	9 ♍
12 ♋	10 ♌	11 ♍	12 ♏	11 ♐	10 ♑	9 ♒	11 ♈	11 ♊	11 ♋	12 ♍	12 ♎
14 ♌	13 ♍	13 ♎	14 ♐	13 ♑	12 ♒	11 ♓	13 ♉	13 ♋	13 ♌	14 ♎	14 ♏
17 ♍	15 ♎	16 ♏	16 ♑	15 ♒	14 ♓	13 ♈	15 ♊	16 ♌	16 ♍	16 ♏	16 ♐
19 ♎	17 ♏	18 ♐	18 ♒	18 ♓	16 ♈	15 ♉	18 ♋	18 ♍	18 ♎	19 ♐	18 ♑
21 ♏	19 ♐	20 ♑	20 ♓	20 ♈	18 ♉	18 ♊	20 ♌	21 ♎	21 ♏	21 ♑	20 ♒
23 ♐	22 ♑	22 ♒	23 ♈	22 ♉	21 ♊	21 ♋	22 ♍	23 ♏	23 ♐	23 ♒	22 ♓
25 ♑	24 ♒	24 ♓	25 ♉	25 ♊	23 ♋	23 ♌	25 ♎	25 ♐	25 ♑	25 ♓	24 ♈
27 ♒	26 ♓	26 ♈	27 ♊	27 ♋	26 ♌	26 ♍	27 ♏	27 ♑	27 ♒	27 ♈	27 ♉
29 ♓	28 ♈	29 ♉	30 ♋	30 ♌	28 ♍	28 ♎	29 ♐	29 ♒	29 ♓	29 ♉	29 ♊
		31 ♊				30 ♏	31 ♑		31 ♈		

1961

JAN.	FEB.	MAR.	APR.	MAY	JUNE	JULY	AUG.	SEPT.	OCT.	NOV.	DEC.
1 ♋	2 ♍	1 ♍	2 ♏	2 ♐	2 ♒	2 ♓	2 ♉	1 ♊	3 ♌	2 ♍	2 ♎
3 ♌	4 ♎	4 ♎	4 ♐	4 ♑	4 ♓	4 ♈	4 ♊	3 ♋	5 ♍	4 ♎	4 ♏
6 ♍	7 ♏	6 ♏	7 ♑	6 ♒	6 ♈	6 ♉	7 ♋	6 ♌	8 ♎	7 ♏	6 ♐
8 ♎	9 ♐	8 ♐	9 ♒	8 ♓	9 ♉	8 ♊	9 ♌	8 ♍	10 ♏	9 ♐	9 ♑
10 ♏	11 ♑	10 ♑	11 ♓	10 ♈	11 ♊	11 ♋	12 ♍	11 ♎	13 ♐	11 ♑	11 ♒
13 ♐	13 ♒	12 ♒	13 ♈	12 ♉	13 ♋	13 ♌	14 ♎	13 ♏	15 ♑	13 ♒	13 ♓
15 ♑	15 ♓	15 ♓	15 ♉	15 ♊	16 ♌	15 ♍	17 ♏	16 ♐	17 ♒	16 ♓	15 ♈
17 ♒	17 ♈	17 ♈	17 ♊	17 ♋	18 ♍	18 ♎	19 ♐	18 ♑	19 ♓	18 ♈	17 ♉
19 ♓	19 ♉	19 ♉	20 ♋	20 ♌	21 ♎	21 ♏	21 ♑	20 ♒	21 ♈	20 ♉	19 ♊
21 ♈	22 ♊	21 ♊	22 ♌	22 ♍	23 ♏	23 ♐	23 ♒	22 ♓	23 ♉	22 ♊	22 ♋
23 ♉	24 ♋	23 ♋	25 ♍	25 ♎	26 ♐	25 ♑	25 ♓	24 ♈	25 ♊	24 ♋	24 ♌
25 ♊	27 ♌	26 ♌	27 ♎	27 ♏	28 ♑	27 ♒	27 ♈	26 ♉	28 ♋	27 ♌	26 ♍
28 ♋		28 ♍	30 ♏	29 ♐	30 ♒	29 ♓	28 ♉	28 ♊	30 ♌	29 ♍	29 ♎
30 ♌		31 ♎		31 ♑		31 ♈		30 ♋			31 ♏

1962

JAN.	FEB.	MAR.	APR.	MAY	JUNE	JULY	AUG.	SEPT.	OCT.	NOV.	DEC.
3 ♐	1 ♑	1 ♑	1 ♓	1 ♈	1 ♊	1 ♋	2 ♍	1 ♎	3 ♐	2 ♑	1 ♒
5 ♑	3 ♒	3 ♒	3 ♈	3 ♉	3 ♋	3 ♌	4 ♎	3 ♏	5 ♑	4 ♒	3 ♓
7 ♒	5 ♓	5 ♓	5 ♉	5 ♊	6 ♌	6 ♍	7 ♏	6 ♐	8 ♒	6 ♓	5 ♈
9 ♓	7 ♈	7 ♈	7 ♊	7 ♋	8 ♍	8 ♎	9 ♐	8 ♑	10 ♓	8 ♈	8 ♉
11 ♈	10 ♉	9 ♉	10 ♋	9 ♌	11 ♎	11 ♏	12 ♑	10 ♒	12 ♈	10 ♉	10 ♊
13 ♉	12 ♊	11 ♊	12 ♌	12 ♍	13 ♏	13 ♐	14 ♒	12 ♓	14 ♉	12 ♊	12 ♋
16 ♊	14 ♋	13 ♋	15 ♍	14 ♎	16 ♐	15 ♑	16 ♓	14 ♈	16 ♊	14 ♋	14 ♌
18 ♋	17 ♌	16 ♌	17 ♎	17 ♏	18 ♑	17 ♒	18 ♈	16 ♉	18 ♋	17 ♌	16 ♍
20 ♌	19 ♍	18 ♍	20 ♏	19 ♐	20 ♒	19 ♓	20 ♉	18 ♊	20 ♌	19 ♍	19 ♎
23 ♍	22 ♎	21 ♎	22 ♐	22 ♑	22 ♓	22 ♈	22 ♊	21 ♋	23 ♍	21 ♎	21 ♏
25 ♎	24 ♏	23 ♏	24 ♑	24 ♒	24 ♈	24 ♉	25 ♋	23 ♌	25 ♎	24 ♏	24 ♐
28 ♏	26 ♐	26 ♐	27 ♒	26 ♓	26 ♉	26 ♊	27 ♌	25 ♍	28 ♏	26 ♐	26 ♑
30 ♐		28 ♑	29 ♓	28 ♈	29 ♊	28 ♋	29 ♍	28 ♎	30 ♐	29 ♑	28 ♒
		30 ♒		30 ♉		30 ♌		30 ♏			31 ♓

1963

JAN.	FEB.	MAR.	APR.	MAY	JUNE	JULY	AUG.	SEPT.	OCT.	NOV.	DEC.
2 ♈	2 ♊	1 ♊	2 ♌	2 ♍	1 ♎	3 ♐	2 ♑	3 ♓	2 ♈	1 ♉	2 ♋
4 ♉	4 ♋	4 ♋	5 ♍	4 ♎	3 ♏	5 ♑	4 ♒	5 ♈	4 ♉	3 ♊	4 ♌
6 ♊	7 ♌	6 ♌	7 ♎	7 ♏	6 ♐	8 ♒	6 ♓	7 ♉	6 ♊	5 ♋	6 ♍
8 ♋	9 ♍	8 ♍	10 ♏	9 ♐	8 ♑	10 ♓	8 ♈	9 ♊	8 ♋	7 ♌	9 ♎
10 ♌	11 ♎	11 ♎	12 ♐	12 ♑	10 ♒	12 ♈	10 ♉	11 ♋	10 ♌	9 ♍	11 ♏
13 ♍	14 ♏	13 ♏	15 ♑	14 ♒	13 ♓	14 ♉	13 ♊	13 ♌	13 ♍	11 ♎	14 ♐
15 ♎	16 ♐	16 ♐	17 ♒	16 ♓	15 ♈	16 ♊	15 ♋	15 ♍	15 ♎	14 ♏	16 ♑
18 ♏	19 ♑	18 ♑	19 ♓	18 ♈	17 ♉	18 ♋	17 ♌	18 ♎	18 ♏	16 ♐	19 ♒
20 ♐	21 ♒	21 ♒	21 ♈	21 ♉	19 ♊	21 ♌	20 ♍	20 ♏	20 ♐	19 ♑	21 ♓
22 ♑	23 ♓	23 ♓	23 ♉	23 ♊	21 ♋	23 ♍	23 ♎	23 ♐	23 ♑	21 ♒	23 ♈
25 ♒	25 ♈	25 ♈	25 ♊	25 ♋	23 ♌	25 ♎	25 ♏	25 ♑	25 ♒	24 ♓	25 ♉
27 ♓	27 ♉	27 ♉	27 ♋	27 ♌	25 ♍	28 ♏	27 ♐	28 ♒	27 ♓	26 ♈	27 ♊
29 ♈		29 ♊	29 ♌	29 ♍	28 ♎	30 ♐	29 ♑	30 ♓	30 ♈	28 ♉	29 ♋
31 ♉		31 ♋		30 ♏	30 ♏		31 ♒			30 ♊	31 ♌

1964

JAN.	FEB.	MAR.	APR.	MAY	JUNE	JULY	AUG.	SEPT.	OCT.	NOV.	DEC.
3 ♍	1 ♎	2 ♏	1 ♐	1 ♑	2 ♓	2 ♊	2 ♋	1 ♋	2 ♍	1 ♎	3 ♐
5 ♎	4 ♏	5 ♐	3 ♑	3 ♒	4 ♈	4 ♋	4 ♌	3 ♌	4 ♎	3 ♏	5 ♑
7 ♏	6 ♐	7 ♑	6 ♒	6 ♓	6 ♉	6 ♌	6 ♍	5 ♍	7 ♏	5 ♐	8 ♒
10 ♐	9 ♑	10 ♒	8 ♓	8 ♈	8 ♊	8 ♍	8 ♎	7 ♎	9 ♐	8 ♑	10 ♓
12 ♑	11 ♒	12 ♓	10 ♈	10 ♉	10 ♋	10 ♎	10 ♏	9 ♏	11 ♑	10 ♒	13 ♈
15 ♒	13 ♓	14 ♈	13 ♉	12 ♊	12 ♌	12 ♏	13 ♐	12 ♐	14 ♒	13 ♓	15 ♉
17 ♓	16 ♈	16 ♉	15 ♊	14 ♋	14 ♍	14 ♐	15 ♑	14 ♑	16 ♓	15 ♈	17 ♊
19 ♈	18 ♉	18 ♊	17 ♋	16 ♌	17 ♎	17 ♑	18 ♒	17 ♒	19 ♈	17 ♉	19 ♋
22 ♉	20 ♊	20 ♋	19 ♌	18 ♍	19 ♏	19 ♒	20 ♓	19 ♓	21 ♉	19 ♊	21 ♌
24 ♊	22 ♋	23 ♌	21 ♍	21 ♎	22 ♐	21 ♓	23 ♈	21 ♈	23 ♊	21 ♋	23 ♍
26 ♋	24 ♌	25 ♍	23 ♎	24 ♏	24 ♑	23 ♈	25 ♉	23 ♉	25 ♋	23 ♌	25 ♎
28 ♌	26 ♍	27 ♎	26 ♏	27 ♐	27 ♒	25 ♉	28 ♊	25 ♊	27 ♌	26 ♍	28 ♏
30 ♍	29 ♎	29 ♏	28 ♐	29 ♑	29 ♈	28 ♊	30 ♊	28 ♋	29 ♍	28 ♎	30 ♐
				30 ♒	31 ♉	31 ♋		30 ♌		30 ♏	

1965

JAN.	FEB.	MAR.	APR.	MAY	JUNE	JULY	AUG.	SEPT.	OCT.	NOV.	DEC.
1 ♑	3 ♓	2 ♓	1 ♈	2 ♊	1 ♋	2 ♍	1 ♎	2 ♐	1 ♑	3 ♓	2 ♈
4 ♒	5 ♈	4 ♈	3 ♉	4 ♋	3 ♌	5 ♎	3 ♏	4 ♑	4 ♒	5 ♈	5 ♉
6 ♓	7 ♉	7 ♉	5 ♊	7 ♌	5 ♍	7 ♏	5 ♐	6 ♒	6 ♓	7 ♉	7 ♊
9 ♈	10 ♊	9 ♊	7 ♋	9 ♍	7 ♎	9 ♐	8 ♑	9 ♓	9 ♈	10 ♊	9 ♋
11 ♉	12 ♋	11 ♋	9 ♌	11 ♎	9 ♏	11 ♑	10 ♒	11 ♈	11 ♉	12 ♋	11 ♌
13 ♊	14 ♌	13 ♌	11 ♍	13 ♏	12 ♐	14 ♒	13 ♓	14 ♉	13 ♊	14 ♌	13 ♍
15 ♋	16 ♍	15 ♍	14 ♎	15 ♐	14 ♑	16 ♓	15 ♈	16 ♊	16 ♋	16 ♍	15 ♎
17 ♌	18 ♎	17 ♎	16 ♏	18 ♑	16 ♒	19 ♈	17 ♉	18 ♋	18 ♌	18 ♎	18 ♏
19 ♍	20 ♏	19 ♏	18 ♐	20 ♒	19 ♓	21 ♉	20 ♊	20 ♌	20 ♍	20 ♏	20 ♐
21 ♎	22 ♐	22 ♐	21 ♑	23 ♓	22 ♈	23 ♊	22 ♋	22 ♍	22 ♎	23 ♐	22 ♑
24 ♏	25 ♑	24 ♑	23 ♒	25 ♈	24 ♉	25 ♋	24 ♌	25 ♎	24 ♏	25 ♑	25 ♒
26 ♐	27 ♒	27 ♒	26 ♓	28 ♉	26 ♊	27 ♌	26 ♍	27 ♏	26 ♐	27 ♒	27 ♓
29 ♑		29 ♓	28 ♈	30 ♊	28 ♋	29 ♍	28 ♎	29 ♐	29 ♑	30 ♓	30 ♈
31 ♒			30 ♉		30 ♌		30 ♏		31 ♒		

1966

JAN.	FEB.	MAR.	APR.	MAY	JUNE	JULY	AUG.	SEPT.	OCT.	NOV.	DEC.
1 ♉	2 ♋	1 ♋	2 ♍	1 ♎	2 ♐	1 ♑	3 ♓	1 ♈	1 ♉	2 ♋	2 ♌
4 ♊	4 ♌	4 ♌	4 ♎	3 ♏	4 ♑	4 ♒	5 ♈	4 ♉	4 ♊	4 ♌	4 ♍
6 ♋	6 ♍	6 ♍	6 ♏	6 ♐	7 ♒	6 ♓	8 ♉	6 ♊	6 ♋	7 ♍	6 ♎
8 ♌	8 ♎	7 ♎	8 ♐	8 ♑	9 ♓	9 ♈	10 ♊	9 ♋	8 ♌	9 ♎	8 ♏
10 ♍	10 ♏	10 ♏	10 ♑	10 ♒	12 ♈	11 ♉	12 ♋	11 ♌	10 ♍	11 ♏	10 ♐
12 ♎	12 ♐	12 ♐	13 ♒	13 ♓	14 ♉	14 ♊	14 ♌	13 ♍	12 ♎	13 ♐	12 ♑
14 ♏	15 ♑	14 ♑	15 ♓	15 ♈	16 ♊	16 ♋	16 ♍	15 ♎	11 ♏	15 ♑	15 ♒
16 ♐	17 ♒	17 ♒	18 ♈	18 ♉	19 ♋	18 ♌	18 ♎	17 ♏	16 ♐	17 ♒	17 ♓
19 ♑	20 ♓	19 ♓	20 ♉	20 ♊	21 ♌	20 ♍	20 ♏	19 ♐	19 ♑	20 ♓	20 ♈
21 ♒	22 ♈	22 ♈	23 ♊	22 ♋	23 ♍	22 ♎	23 ♐	21 ♑	21 ♒	22 ♈	22 ♉
24 ♓	25 ♉	24 ♉	25 ♋	24 ♌	25 ♎	24 ♏	25 ♑	24 ♒	23 ♓	25 ♉	25 ♊
26 ♈	27 ♊	26 ♊	27 ♌	26 ♍	27 ♏	26 ♐	27 ♒	26 ♓	26 ♈	27 ♊	27 ♋
29 ♉		29 ♋	29 ♍	29 ♎	29 ♐	29 ♑	30 ♓	29 ♈	28 ♉	29 ♋	29 ♌
31 ♊		31 ♌		31 ♏		31 ♒			31 ♊		31 ♍

1967

JAN.	FEB.	MAR.	APR.	MAY	JUNE	JULY	AUG.	SEPT.	OCT.	NOV.	DEC.
2 ♎	1 ♏	2 ♐	1 ♑	3 ♓	1 ♈	1 ♉	2 ♋	1 ♌	1 ♍	1 ♏	1 ♐
4 ♏	3 ♐	4 ♑	3 ♒	5 ♈	4 ♉	4 ♊	5 ♌	3 ♍	3 ♎	3 ♐	3 ♑
7 ♐	5 ♑	7 ♒	5 ♓	8 ♉	6 ♊	6 ♋	7 ♍	5 ♎	5 ♏	5 ♐	5 ♒
9 ♑	7 ♒	9 ♓	8 ♈	10 ♊	9 ♋	8 ♌	9 ♎	7 ♏	7 ♐	7 ♑	7 ♓
11 ♒	10 ♓	12 ♈	10 ♉	12 ♋	11 ♌	11 ♍	11 ♏	9 ♐	9 ♑	10 ♒	9 ♈
13 ♓	12 ♈	14 ♉	13 ♊	15 ♌	13 ♍	13 ♎	13 ♐	12 ♑	11 ♒	12 ♓	12 ♉
16 ♈	15 ♉	17 ♊	15 ♋	17 ♍	15 ♎	15 ♏	15 ♑	14 ♒	13 ♓	15 ♈	14 ♊
18 ♉	17 ♊	19 ♋	18 ♌	19 ♎	18 ♏	17 ♐	18 ♒	16 ♓	16 ♈	17 ♉	17 ♋
21 ♊	20 ♋	21 ♌	20 ♍	21 ♏	20 ♐	19 ♑	20 ♓	19 ♈	18 ♉	20 ♊	19 ♌
23 ♋	22 ♌	23 ♍	22 ♎	23 ♐	22 ♑	21 ♒	22 ♈	21 ♉	21 ♊	22 ♋	22 ♍
25 ♌	24 ♍	25 ♎	24 ♏	25 ♑	24 ♒	24 ♓	25 ♉	24 ♊	23 ♋	24 ♌	24 ♎
27 ♍	26 ♎	27 ♏	26 ♐	27 ♒	26 ♓	26 ♈	27 ♊	26 ♋	26 ♌	27 ♎	26 ♏
30 ♎	28 ♏	29 ♐	28 ♑	30 ♓	29 ♈	29 ♉	30 ♋	28 ♌	28 ♍	29 ♏	28 ♐
			30 ♒			31 ♊			30 ♎		30 ♑

1968

JAN.	FEB.	MAR.	APR.	MAY	JUNE	JULY	AUG.	SEPT.	OCT.	NOV.	DEC.
1 ♒	2 ♈	3 ♉	2 ♊	2 ♋	3 ♍	2 ♎	1 ♏	1 ♑	3 ♓	1 ♈	1 ♉
3 ♓	5 ♉	5 ♊	4 ♋	4 ♌	5 ♎	4 ♏	3 ♐	3 ♒	5 ♈	4 ♉	3 ♊
6 ♈	7 ♊	8 ♋	7 ♌	6 ♍	7 ♏	6 ♐	5 ♑	5 ♓	7 ♉	6 ♊	6 ♋
8 ♉	10 ♋	10 ♌	9 ♍	9 ♎	9 ♐	8 ♑	7 ♒	8 ♈	10 ♊	9 ♋	8 ♌
11 ♊	12 ♌	13 ♍	11 ♎	11 ♏	11 ♑	10 ♒	9 ♓	10 ♉	12 ♋	11 ♌	11 ♍
13 ♋	14 ♍	15 ♎	13 ♏	13 ♐	13 ♒	12 ♓	11 ♈	12 ♊	15 ♌	14 ♍	13 ♎
16 ♌	16 ♎	17 ♏	15 ♐	15 ♑	15 ♓	15 ♈	14 ♉	15 ♋	17 ♍	16 ♎	15 ♏
18 ♍	18 ♏	19 ♐	17 ♑	17 ♒	18 ♈	17 ♉	16 ♊	17 ♌	19 ♎	18 ♏	17 ♐
20 ♎	21 ♐	21 ♑	19 ♒	19 ♓	20 ♉	20 ♊	19 ♋	20 ♍	22 ♏	20 ♐	19 ♑
22 ♏	23 ♑	23 ♒	22 ♓	21 ♈	23 ♊	22 ♋	21 ♌	22 ♎	24 ♐	22 ♑	21 ♒
24 ♐	25 ♒	25 ♓	24 ♈	23 ♉	25 ♋	25 ♌	24 ♍	24 ♏	26 ♑	24 ♒	23 ♓
26 ♑	27 ♈	28 ♈	27 ♉	25 ♊	28 ♌	27 ♍	26 ♎	26 ♐	28 ♒	26 ♓	26 ♈
29 ♒	29 ♈	30 ♉	29 ♊	28 ♋	30 ♍	29 ♎	28 ♏	28 ♑	30 ♓	28 ♈	28 ♉
31 ♓				31 ♌			30 ♐	30 ♒			31 ♊

1969

JAN.	FEB.	MAR.	APR.	MAY	JUNE	JULY	AUG.	SEPT.	OCT.	NOV.	DEC.
2 ♋	1 ♌	3 ♍	1 ♎	1 ♏	1 ♑	1 ♒	1 ♈	2 ♊	2 ♋	1 ♌	1 ♍
5 ♌	3 ♍	5 ♎	4 ♏	3 ♐	3 ♒	3 ♓	4 ♉	5 ♋	5 ♌	4 ♍	3 ♎
7 ♍	6 ♎	7 ♏	6 ♐	5 ♑	5 ♓	5 ♈	6 ♊	7 ♌	7 ♍	6 ♎	6 ♏
9 ♎	8 ♏	9 ♐	8 ♑	7 ♒	8 ♈	7 ♉	9 ♋	10 ♍	9 ♎	8 ♏	8 ♐
12 ♏	10 ♐	11 ♑	10 ♒	9 ♓	10 ♉	10 ♊	11 ♌	12 ♎	12 ♏	10 ♐	10 ♑
14 ♐	12 ♑	14 ♒	12 ♓	11 ♈	13 ♊	12 ♋	14 ♍	15 ♏	14 ♐	12 ♑	12 ♒
16 ♑	14 ♒	16 ♓	14 ♈	14 ♉	15 ♋	15 ♌	16 ♎	17 ♐	16 ♑	14 ♒	14 ♓
18 ♒	16 ♓	18 ♈	17 ♉	16 ♊	18 ♌	17 ♍	18 ♏	19 ♑	18 ♒	17 ♓	16 ♈
20 ♓	18 ♈	20 ♉	19 ♊	19 ♋	20 ♍	20 ♎	20 ♐	21 ♒	20 ♓	19 ♈	18 ♉
22 ♈	21 ♉	23 ♊	21 ♋	22 ♌	22 ♎	22 ♏	23 ♑	23 ♓	22 ♈	21 ♉	20 ♊
24 ♉	23 ♊	25 ♋	24 ♌	24 ♍	24 ♏	24 ♐	25 ♒	25 ♈	25 ♉	23 ♊	23 ♋
27 ♊	26 ♋	28 ♌	26 ♍	26 ♎	27 ♐	26 ♑	27 ♓	27 ♉	27 ♊	26 ♋	26 ♌
29 ♋	28 ♌	30 ♍	29 ♎	28 ♏	29 ♑	28 ♒	29 ♈	30 ♊	30 ♋	28 ♌	28 ♍
				30 ♐		30 ♓	31 ♉				31 ♎

The Meaning of Your Moon

Moon in Aries — "Now" is the way you like things — immediately if not sooner! Your emotions make you impatient, impulsive, energetic, ambitious. It's hard to bluff you or frighten you because you have so much courage and self-confidence. Tone down your temper and practice self-control.

Moon in Taurus — Your emotions make you a mellow, tranquil soul — but maybe just a bit too stubborn about having your own way. You like beautiful things and it could be that you possess a lovely singing voice. Correct that self-satisfied streak, be flexible instead of sluggish.

Moon in Gemini — This is the sign of the chatterbox, but people love to hear you talk. You're happiest when communicating, whether it's by reading, writing, or rapping. You have the "gift of gab," and don't mind sharing it. What's your problem? Well, sometimes you're too restless to be reliable.

Moon in Cancer — Romantic and impressionable, that's you. Maybe you're too impressionable, so that you have no fixed opinions of your own. Try being yourself — chances are everyone will like it better that way. And watch those swings of mood! You'll find contentment in making the domestic scene.

Moon in Leo — Ambitious and independent, you're also a perfectionist. Everything has got to be just right or it's not good enough for you. Watch that ego, and let your kindness and generosity have the spotlight.

Moon in Virgo — Your head often rules your heart. You're full of common sense, and you're never at a loss for solutions to problems because your mind is sharp and orderly. Neatness counts with you, inside and out. But don't let that love of order make you fussy and fault-finding with those who don't do things just your way.

Moon in Libra — If your moon is here, you probably never lack for dates. You're popular and have a busy social life — probably because you're naturally charming and cooperative. Because you seem so easygoing, some people may try to push you around. Remember, wanting to please can cost too much when it becomes a peace-at-any-price policy. Stick to what you know is right.

Moon in Scorpio — Nobody has to tell you to stand up for yourself. You know what you want out of life and you mean to get it. It's all or nothing at all with you, and sometimes your determination to have your way seems rude and ruthless. Cool it! Tone down those turbulent emotions so that others can see how sympathetic and understanding you really are.

Moon in Sagittarius — To others, you seem to be the original "good sport" — unless you let your nervousness and restlessness show through. Let your sunshine in, and you'll brighten a lot of drab lives and dark corners. You love to be on the go, but pick your destinations and stick to them.

Moon in Capricorn — Everyone counts on you. You're reliable, careful, orderly. But you don't come on as warm as you should — all that reserve makes you seem cold and distant. Try taking the wraps off your emotions and letting them all hang out once in a while. And also try not to be such a stickler for routine in your climb to the top. You'll get there just as fast if you take time out now and then.

Moon in Aquarius — You're a walking declaration of independence, aren't you? Offbeat, original, you like to go your own way and do your own thing. Maybe now and then you also like to prove how different you are by shocking others. Try a little persuasion instead of shock tactics, and get them on your side. Put yourself in the other fellow's shoes more often.

Moon in Pisces — You're a friend in need. You get the message half the time without being told. But sometimes all that emotional input is too much for your shy, sensitive nature, and you look for an escape. Face reality instead of copping out. Daydreams or other "escapes" such as drugs won't get you anywhere. You have the kind of nature that can only help itself by helping others.

What About the Ascendant?

Your "Ascendant" is the zodiac sign that was rising on the Eastern horizon at the moment of your birth. Astrologers say it has a lot to do with the way you look, and the way the world looks to you. It is also supposed to control your mannerisms, attitudes, and temperament. Sometimes called the "Rising Sign," the Ascendant is said to signify your social side — the way in which you relate to other people — the way you "come on" to others. The Ascendant, if astrologers are right, is what's up front. That is why it is often easier to guess someone's Ascendant than his zodiac Sun sign.

To find your Ascendant, look for the date nearest your birthdate in the following tables. Then find the time nearest to the moment you were born. The abbreviation after this time will tell you what your "Rising Sign" is. (Ars means Aries; Tau = Taurus; Gem = Gemini; Can = Cancer; Vir = Virgo; Lib = Libra; Sco = Scorpio; Sag = Sagittarius; Cap = Capricorn; Aqr = Aquarius; Pis = Pisces).

If you don't know the hour of your birth, you have lots of company, so don't worry. Forget about your Ascendant, and just have fun reading about your Sun sign and your Moon sign.

RISING SIGNS OR ASCENDANTS

JAN. 1st Hour:	JAN. 15th Hour:	FEB. 1st Hour:	FEB. 15th Hour:
12:25 AM—Lib	2:00 AM—Sco	1:00 AM—Sco	12:10 AM—Sco
3:00 AM—Sco	4:30 AM—Sag	3:30 AM—Sag	2:30 AM—Sag
5:30 AM—Sag	6:45 AM—Cap	5:45 AM—Cap	4:45 AM—Cap
7:40 AM—Cap	8:15 AM—Aqr	7:15 AM—Aqr	6:20 AM—Aqr
9:20 AM—Aqr	9:40 AM—Pis	8:40 AM—Pis	7:40 AM—Pis
10:40 AM—Pis	10:35 AM—Ars	9:50 AM—Ars	8:50 AM—Ars
11:50 AM—Ars	12:05 PM—Tau	11:05 AM—Tau	10:05 AM—Tau
1:05 PM—Tau	1:45 PM—Gem	12:45 PM—Gem	11:40 AM—Gem
2:40 PM—Gem	3:55 PM—Can	3:00 PM—Can	2:00 PM—Can
5:00 PM—Can	6:25 PM—Leo	5:20 PM—Leo	4:25 PM—Leo
7:25 PM—Leo	9:00 PM—Vir	8:00 PM—Vir	7:00 PM—Vir
10:00 PM—Vir	11:25 PM—Lib	10:25 PM—Lib	9:45 PM—Lib

MAR. 1st	MAR. 16th	APR. 1st	APR. 16th
Hour:	Hour:	Hour:	Hour:
1:25 AM—Sag	12:30 AM—Sag	1:45 AM—Cap	12:25 AM—Cap
3:45 AM—Cap	2:45 AM—Cap	3:20 AM—Aqr	2:55 AM—Aqr
5:20 AM—Aqr	4:20 AM—Aqr	4:40 AM—Pis	3:40 AM—Pis
6:40 AM—Pis	5:40 AM—Pis	5:55 AM—Ars	4:50 AM—Ars
7:50 AM—Ars	6:50 AM—Ars	7:10 AM—Tau	6:05 AM—Tau
9:25 AM—Tau	8:05 AM—Tau	8:50 AM—Gem	7:50 AM—Gem
10:45 AM—Gem	9:35 AM—Gem	10:55 AM—Can	10:00 AM—Can
12:55 AM—Can	11:55 AM—Can	1:20 PM—Leo	12:25 PM—Leo
3:25 PM—Leo	2:25 PM—Leo	4:05 PM—Vir	3:10 PM—Vir
6:00 PM—Vir	4:55 PM—Vir	6:20 PM—Lib	5:25 PM—Lib
8:25 PM—Lib	7:25 PM—Lib	9:05 PM—Sco	8:05 PM—Sco
10:55 PM—Sco	9:55 PM—Sco	11:30 PM—Sag	10:45 PM—Sag

MAY 1st	MAY 16th	JUN. 1st	JUN. 16th
Hour:	Hour:	Hour:	Hour:
1:20 AM—Aqr	12:20 AM—Aqr	12:40 AM—Pis	12:50 AM—Ars
2:40 AM—Pis	1:40 AM—Pis	1:50 AM—Ars	2:05 AM—Tau
3:55 AM—Ars	2:45 AM—Ars	3:05 AM—Tau	3:50 AM—Gem
5:05 AM—Tau	4:05 AM—Tau	4:50 AM—Gem	6:00 AM—Can
6:45 AM—Gem	5:40 AM—Gem	7:00 AM—Can	8:25 AM—Leo
9:00 AM—Can	8:00 AM—Can	9:25 AM—Leo	11:00 AM—Vir
11:25 AM—Leo	10:20 AM—Leo	11:55 AM—Vir	1:25 PM—Lib
2:00 PM—Vir	1:00 PM—Vir	2:25 PM—Lib	4:00 PM—Sco
4:25 PM—Lib	3:25 PM—Lib	4:55 PM—Sco	6:25 PM—Sag
7:05 PM—Sco	6:00 PM—Sco	7:25 PM—Sag	8:45 PM—Cap
9:30 PM—Sag	8:25 PM—Sag	9:45 PM—Cap	10:15 PM—Aqr
11:45 PM—Cap	10:45 PM—Cap	11:20 PM—Aqr	11:35 PM—Pis

JUL. 1st	JUL. 16th	AUG. 1st	AUG. 16th
Hour:	Hour:	Hour:	Hour:
1:05 AM—Tau	12:05 AM—Tau	12:45 AM—Gem	2:00 AM—Can
2:45 AM—Gem	1:35 AM—Gem	3:00 AM—Can	4:25 AM—Leo
5:10 AM—Can	4:00 AM—Can	5:25 AM—Leo	7:00 AM—Vir
7:25 AM—Leo	6:25 AM—Leo	8:10 AM—Vir	9:25 AM—Lib
10:00 AM—Vir	9:00 AM—Vir	10:25 AM—Lib	NOON—Sco
12:25 PM—Lib	11:25 AM—Lib	12:55 PM—Sco	2:30 PM—Sag
3:05 PM—Sco	2:00 PM—Sco	3:40 PM—Sag	4:45 PM—Cap
5:30 PM—Sag	4:25 PM—Sag	5:45 PM—Cap	6:15 PM—Aqr
7:45 PM—Cap	6:45 PM—Cap	7:20 PM—Aqr	7:40 PM—Pis
9:20 PM—Aqr	8:20 PM—Aqr	8:35 PM—Pis	8:50 PM—Ars
10:40 PM—Pis	9:40 PM—Pis	9:55 PM—Ars	10:05 PM—Tau
11:50 PM—Ars	10:50 PM—Ars	11:05 PM—Tau	11:40 PM—Gem

SEP. 1st	SEP. 16th	OCT. 1st	OCT. 16th
Hour:	Hour:	Hour:	Hour:
1:10 AM—Can	12 MIDNT—Can	1:20 AM—Leo	12:25 AM—Leo
3:25 AM—Leo	2:30 AM—Leo	4:10 AM—Vir	2:55 AM—Vir
5:55 AM—Vir	4:55 AM—Vir	6:25 AM—Lib	5:20 AM—Lib
8:25 AM—Lib	7:20 AM—Lib	8:55 AM—Sco	7:55 AM—Sco
11:05 AM—Sco	10:00 AM—Sco	11:30 AM—Sag	10:30 AM—Sag
1:30 PM—Sag	12:25 PM—Sag	1:45 PM—Cap	12:35 PM—Cap
3:45 PM—Cap	2:45 PM—Cap	3:20 PM—Aqr	2:15 PM—Aqr
5:15 PM—Aqr	4:20 PM—Aqr	4:40 PM—Pis	3:40 PM—Pis
6:40 PM—Pis	5:40 PM—Pis	5:50 PM—Ars	4:55 PM—Ars
7:50 PM—Ars	6:50 PM—Ars	7:05 PM—Tau	6:05 PM—Tau
9:00 PM—Tau	8:05 PM—Tau	8:55 PM—Gem	7:40 PM—Gem
10:55 PM—Gem	9:55 PM—Gem	10:55 PM—Can	10:15 PM—Can

NOV. 1st	NOV. 16th	DEC. 1st	DEC. 16th
Hour:	Hour:	Hour:	Hour:
1:55 AM—Vir	12:55 AM—Vir	12 MIDNT—Vir	1:25 AM—Lib
4:20 AM—Lib	3:25 AM—Lib	2:25 AM—Lib	3:55 AM—Sco
6:55 AM—Sco	5:55 AM—Sco	4:55 AM—Sco	6:25 AM—Sag
9:35 AM—Sag	8:25 AM—Sag	7:30 AM—Sag	8:45 AM—Cap
11:40 AM—Cap	10:45 AM—Cap	9:45 AM—Cap	10:15 AM—Aqr
1:20 PM—Aqr	12:15 PM—Aqr	11:20 AM—Aqr	11:40 AM—Pis
2:35 PM—Pis	1:40 PM—Pis	12:35 PM—Pis	12:45 PM—Ars
3:40 PM—Ars	2:50 PM—Ars	1:45 PM—Ars	2:05 PM—Tau
5:15 PM—Tau	4:05 PM—Tau	3:00 PM—Tau	3:55 PM—Gem
6:45 PM—Gem	5:40 PM—Gem	4:40 PM—Gem	5:55 PM—Can
9:10 PM—Can	8:10 PM—Can	6:55 PM—Can	8:35 PM—Leo
11:25 PM—Leo	10:25 PM—Leo	9:35 PM—Leo	11:10 PM—Vir

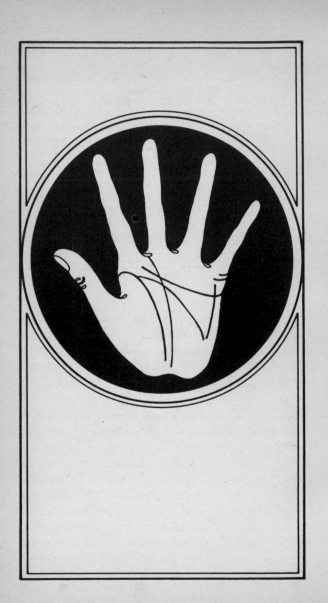

PALMISTRY – YOUR FORTUNE IN HAND

Palmistry is a real hand-me-down, for people have been puzzling over the meaning of the lines on the human palm for centuries. The real puzzle lies in the fact that although everyone has lines on the palms of their hands — no two palm prints are alike! A palm print is as individual as a fingerprint. No one else in the world has the same lines in the same places on their palms as you do.

What do these mysterious lines on your palms mean? Scientists and doctors now think that they may offer clues to your health and your tendency to certain diseases. But for thousands of years many people have believed that the lines in the human hand were a kind of "writing" which could tell a great deal about character, talents — and perhaps even the person's future!

Gypsy fortune-tellers have pointed out that the lines on the hand sometimes change. Do they change as our fortunes change? Do new ones appear to mark our successes or failures? Do old ones vanish to show that certain phases in our lives are completed? No one knows the reasons for these changing lines for certain, but prints taken of hands from childhood to old age show that these changes do take place.

According to palmists, the left hand shows the

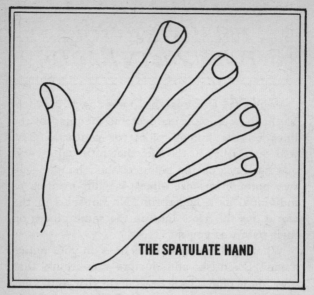

THE SPATULATE HAND

characteristics with which you were born. The lines on the left hand are supposed to reveal your fears, ambitions, and desires.

The right hand has a different story to tell. Here, say the palmists, can be seen what's happening in the present — and what *could* happen in the future. Are you going to get married, go to college, be drafted? Will you succeed or fail? It's all supposed to be there in your right hand.

Before we check out the lines on your palms, let's take a look at the shape of your hands. Put your palms down on some surface, and look at the backs of your hands. Are they large and broad, with short strong fingers with broad tips? Is the base sort of spade-shaped, narrower than the top of the palm? If so, you have a *spatulate*

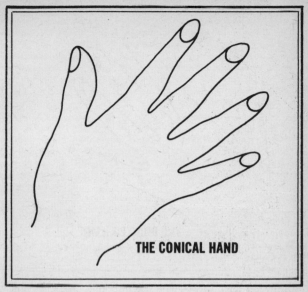

THE CONICAL HAND

hand, and your motto is Go! Go! Go! You would rather think than act, but you have a lot of intuition that helps you out of the scrapes your adventurous spirit gets you into. You are energetic and daring, a true pioneer. Owners of *spatulate* hands are said to be good engineers, nurses, secretaries, builders, scientists, generals, and business executives. You might even be a mechanical genius!

Here are some other hand shapes, and the clues they provide to character:

Conical: The base is broad, narrowing up toward the fingers. The fingers taper, narrow at the tips and thick at the base. *Conical* hand owners are said to be good-natured, sympathetic, diplomatic, adaptable, and impulsive. If the

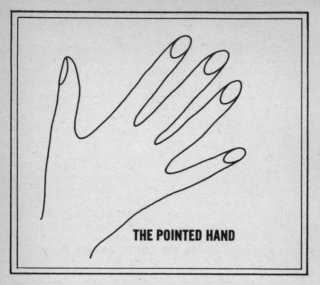

THE POINTED HAND

knuckles are large, the owner has gifts as an inventor or philosopher. If they are small, he (or she) could be an actor, lawyer, designer, writer, or broadcaster.

Pointed: This is the so-called "almond-shaped" hand, rounded at the base and tapering upward into smooth, pointed fingers. Owners of these hands want to beautify their surroundings, and they often become designers, beauticians, musicians, or artists. Some of them can even be found in front of movie cameras, or in back of them as directors. The more prominent the knuckles on the pointed hand, the harder the owner will work to bring beauty into his life.

It could be that your hand doesn't fit any of these descriptions. Perhaps it is a kind of oblong

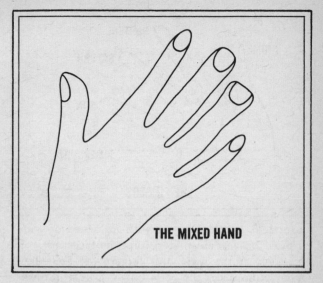

THE MIXED HAND

shape, round at the base of the palm and squared off at the base of the fingers. If this is the case, you have what is called the *mixed* hand, and you are probably both practical and creative, dependable and hard-working. The only thing you have to watch out for is your red-hot temper. You'll be happiest in such professions as journalism, teaching, architecture, medicine, or politics.

How about your fingers? Their shapes have something to say about your character too.

Short fingers — an energetic, driving nature. *Long fingers* — less energy, more nervousness, patience, and ambition. *Square fingers* (straight and squared off at tips) — careful, hard-working, slow to make up your mind. *Pointed fingers* (tapered at the tips) — sensitive, idealistic, im-

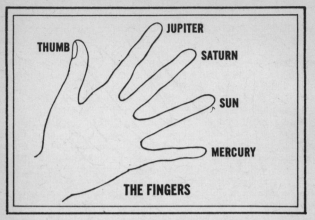

THE FINGERS

practical, poetic. Fingers with *flattened or wide tips* — brave, determined, impatient, restless.

Look at the way your fingers are joined to your palm. Does the little finger start at a lower point than the first finger? If so, you will have to work hard to get what you want. Life will be a struggle, but you'll make it.

Each finger is associated with a planet, which shows palmistry's link to astrology, and is said to have the characteristics of that planet:

First finger: Ruled by Jupiter, associated with knowledge, justice, and intelligence. Is it long? — You want to be first in everything. Short? You probably would rather not lead — too much responsibility. Crooked? You know how to use any situation to make yourself look good.

Second finger: Ruled by Saturn, associated with self-discipline, plus what our efforts and personal experience bring us. Long — maybe you're too impetuous. Short — look before you

70

leap, you're too impetuous. Well-developed —
you're the serious type, but you're well-balanced.
Crooked — you worry too much.

Third finger: Ruled by the sun, associated
with creative abilities and self-expression. Long
— you could get wealthy. Almost as long as
the second finger — you might gamble your
wealth away. Crooked — you'll do almost anything to make money. Balanced and well-formed
— you probably have literary or artistic talent.

Fourth (or little) finger: Ruled by the planet Mercury, associated with the way you use
your brain and your hands. Is your little finger
straight? If so, you've got talent, and you know
how to develop and use it. But if it's crooked,
watch your tendency to be too outspoken and
brusque. You need to learn that more flies can
be caught with the honey of diplomacy. If your
little finger is long, you don't care how many
obstacles are set up in your way. You regard
them as a challenge, and climb right over them.
The opposite is true if the little finger is short.

The thumb: Check out the length of your
thumb. Does it reach (or nearly reach) the
first joint of your first finger? If it does, you've
got a will of iron and willpower to match. (The
top joint of the thumb represents your will.)

If this top (or first) joint of your thumb is
longer than the second joint, you're reliable, re-
sponsible, strong-willed — and perhaps a little
self-centered. If this joint is bulgy and too de-
veloped, you could be on a real ego trip all the
time. But if it's just slightly wide at the top,
you're creative and imaginative.

The second joint of the thumb rules the ability to reason logically. The longer this joint, the more clear-headed and logical you are. But if it is much longer than the top joint, you may lack the will power to carry out those groovy ideas.

Now spread your hand, moving your thumb away from the other fingers as far as it will go. The wider the spread, the more generous you are. If the spread is small and tight-looking, you may be almost too thrifty by nature.

No fingers are complete without fingernails, and most nails have a speck of white on them from time to time. If these white specks seem to be permanent, they have meanings all their own. Gypsy fortune-tellers say specks on the thumbnail mean much travel; on the first fingernail, powerful enemies; on the second fingernail, an up-and-down life with lots of changes; on the third fingernail, more worries than you need; and on the little fingernail, you get lucky just when you need to.

THE MOUNDS

What's a mound? It's one of the little pads on the palm just below the fingers. You may have a flat mound under one finger, and a plump one under another. According to palmists, the flatness or fullness of a mound tells a lot about you.

The Mound of Mercury lies beneath the little

finger. If it's well-developed, you'll be healthy and successful in business. It also shows good-nature, enthusiasm, and a sense of humor. However, if it's very large — larger than any of the other mounds, for example — and full, you may try to get what you want by underhanded means. Remember, honesty is still the best policy. Little up and down lines on this mound mean you ought to choose a career that will enable you to help people.

The Mound of Apollo is just under the third or "ring" finger. If it's plump and well-developed, you are interested in the arts and also in people. You like a lively social life, but if this mound is too broad and too soft, you may spend too much time daydreaming about what you want instead of working to get it. An undeveloped Mound of Apollo means a person full of common sense, but lacking imagination and appreciation of the arts.

Are there little up and down lines on this mound? This is supposed to mean you'll have an artistic career, and make money out of it. Is there a "cross" (one tiny line bisecting another) on it? This could mean a disappointment if you try for a career in the arts. Do four tiny lines form a "square" on this mound? If so, nothing stops you. You'll push and shove your way to the top.

The Mound of Saturn is under the middle finger, and it rules your moods, your courage, and the secret you. If it's well-developed, you're practically fearless. You're also the moody, let-me-alone type.

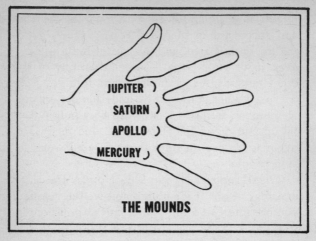

JUPITER)
SATURN)
APOLLO)
MERCURY)

THE MOUNDS

Palmists say the less well-developed the Mound of Saturn, the better. People with a large one tend to want to shut out the world. If the Heart Line touches this mound, you'd better watch those selfish tendencies. But if it is touched by the Line of Fate, nothing gets you down for long. You take what comes without complaining.

The Mound of Jupiter is under the first (or index) finger. It shows how you feel about others, and what position you'll hold in life. It it's well-developed, expect a happy, useful life. But if it's too large, too broad and soft, you could be conceited, extravagant, and too fond of taking things in an easy way. If the Heart Line touches this mound, everything you do seems to turn to money. And if your Life Line hooks onto the Mound of Jupiter, you're very, very ambitious. Then there's the Fate Line. Let it join the Mound of Jupiter, and you're a shoo-in for success.

THE MAIN LINES

Circling around the thumb is the *Life Line*. If it is long, well-marked, and unbroken, you'll have a long life and good health. Breaks in the life line usually mean illnesses or accidents. But unless these breaks show up in the same place on both hands, they'll be minor setbacks.

Does your Life Line end near the wrist in a little fork? That's good, for it foretells a long, active, and vigorous life.

Does a line rise up from your Life Line to the Mound of Jupiter? Good! It's a sign of success.

Does the Life Line join the Head Line at its start? You're shy and sensitive, but you gain self-confidence as time goes on. This is also supposed to mean that you're a fatalist — the kind of a person who accepts what happens with "What will be, will be." Don't give in too easily. A little effort on your part could change things. If your Life Line doesn't touch the Head Line, but just runs parallel to it, you are probably brave and self-confident.

Let's say your Life Line doesn't swing down toward the wrist, as most do, but runs outward toward the other side of your palm. If this is the case, you'd better always keep a suitcase packed. You're going to be traveling most of the time. And when you're not traveling, you'll be moving, changing your residence frequently.

The Head Line starts near the top of the Life Line and keeps going across the palm. If it slopes down into the palm, you're sensitive and imaginative. If it runs in a straight line out from

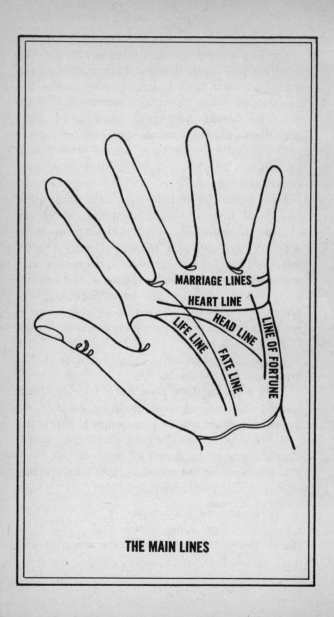

MARRIAGE LINES

HEART LINE

HEAD LINE

LINE OF FORTUNE

LIFE LINE

FATE LINE

THE MAIN LINES

its starting point, you've got the kind of mind that will make you an "A" student. In fact, the longer the Head Line, the brighter its owner, say palmists. If it's long enough to reach the outer edge of the palm, its owner is practically a genius. Long, deep, and strong, it means a logical mind plus a total recall kind of memory.

You can be just as intelligent if your Head Line is faint and wavery, but your memory and powers of concentration won't be as good. And if your Head Line is short, you probably act first and think later. If the Head Line is short and very deep and clear, it means a go-getter who bulldozes his way through obstacles.

Some people have long swooping Head Lines that turn upward toward the middle of the palm. This is the sign of the collector — of facts as well as things. It is also a sign of an elephantlike memory.

Perhaps your Head Line is short and up-turning? You try to go in too many directions at once with the result that people think you're a scatterbrain. Is this line long and downturning? You've got almost too much imagination, but you might try pairing it with that creative talent.

A break in a Head Line means a change — usually in mental outlook. "Chains" (lines that look like connected loops) on a Head Line show a tendency to worry too much. And look at the space between your Head Line and Heart Line. The wider the space, the more broad-minded you are.

The Heart Line runs across the palm just above the Head Line. It begins either under the first or second finger, and then shoots across the palm to end under or near the little finger. It rules your ability to give and receive love.

If the Heart Line starts near you first finger, you'll be lucky in marriage and love. If it starts on the Mound of Jupiter, you're all heart. In fact, you probably wear your heart on your sleeve and give it away all too easily.

Some Heart Lines begin under the second finger. That means that you have a hard time expressing your feelings. People may think you're cold, but the truth is that you're shy.

If your Heart Line dips down to connect with the Head Line, your heart rules your head. If your Heart Line is a double one, with another line running right under it, the one you love will protect and care for you. A "chained" Heart Line (those looplike markings we mentioned under the section on the Head Line) means you're fickle and changeable when it comes to emotions.

Here are some other clues your Heart Line offers:

Long and curved: You're romantic.

Curving upward from the Head Line: You'll give up everything for love.

Straight and parrallel to the Head Line: You've got an iron grip on your emotions. Brains count more than beauty with you, and friendship is more important than romance.

Are there branches on your Heart Line? Does it have a break in it? Brace yourself. You're in for a disappointment in love.

A long Heart Line that runs all the way across the palm, starting just under the first finger, means that its owner puts the person he loves on a pedestal. The one he marries will have a lot to live up to.

Those with Heart Lines that begin under their second fingers sometimes seem to have cash registers for hearts. They are often too materialistic to be romantic.

You're lucky if your Heart Line begins almost at the base of your first finger, for it means you'll have a happy marriage. But should the Heart Line link up with that "ring" line at the base of the first finger, you could marry in haste and repent at leisure.

In some hands, there is only one horizontal line. If that's the case with you, you don't have a Heart Line. When there's only one line running across the palm, it has to be the Head Line. This means that your head will always rule your heart. And that's not all bad!

Marriage Lines. Look at the space just under your little finger. Do you see some short horizontal lines there? These are called Marriage Lines. If they are faint, they stand for romances. But if you see a deep, clear, strong one — that's a happy marriage. And if there are little vertical lines branching up or down from it, these are said to show how many children will be born of the marriage.

Is there a fork on the marriage line at the side nearest your palm? That means a long engagement before marriage.

Does a tiny line cross the marriage line, blocking it off at the end? This could mean a divorce.

Does the marriage line break and then start again? Palmists say this shows that the husband and wife will have separations, but will be reunited.

Is the marriage line close to the Heart Line? You'll be married early in life. Is it high and near the little finger? Marriage will be delayed until late in life.

The Fate Line. The Fate Line starts near the wrist in the middle of the palm. In most hands, it runs up toward the base of the middle finger. If it is very strong and deep in your hand, circumstances are often beyond your control. If it is faint and weak, but combined with a strong Head, Heart, and Life Line, you control your circumstances and make your own luck.

A straight, clear, and unbroken Fate Line means a lucky and successful person. If the Fate Line joins the Life Line at any point, you've got the ability to succeed at whatever you attempt in life. And if your Fate Line begins at your wrist, nothing can stop your climb to the top.

Some Fate Lines break at the Head Line and then start over. This means more than one career, and success at both.

Most Fate Lines end under the second finger, but if yours ends under the first finger, double harness is for you. You will probably marry well, and all partnerships will be lucky for you. If your Fate Line zooms up to end under your third finger, you could be a best-selling author or an acclaimed artist.

Line of Fortune. Not everyone has a Line of Fortune, but if you do, it runs upward near the outside of the palm. A strong, clearly-marked one means you'll be happy and famous in your work.

If the Line of Fortune starts at the Head Line and runs upward through the Heart Line, expect success late in life. If it starts from the Head Line and ends in a fork, you'll have to work hard for what you get — but you'll get it! If it rises to the third finger, it means a career in the arts will bring fame. A Line of Fortune that shows breaks means that sometimes your public will cheer and sometimes they'll jeer — but they'll never ignore you.

Would-Be Palmists, Attention!

There are lots of lines on every palm, and all of them are said to be important. In this chapter we have included only the most easily recognized ones, the so-called "major" lines. If you want to try to "read" these lines, remember to combine their "messages" with the meanings of the shape of the hand and fingers, and the development of the so-called "Mounds."

It is just as important to decide what you want the palm to tell you. If you are trying to find out about talents, abilities, ambitions, desires, and fears, the *left* hand is the one to check out. It is supposed to be the "hand you were born with." But if you seek hints about the present and future, palmists advise you to look at the *right* hand. That one, they say, is the "hand you make by the way you live."

THE TAROT

Tarot cards are really *weird*! As one teenager said, "The pictures on the cards are spooky. They seem to tell you too much, things you would rather not know. They put you in touch with things you can't really think out for yourself."

Many people in many times and places would agree with her. The Tarot has been used to tell fortunes for a very long time. No one is sure just how long. Cleopatra is supposed to have used a Tarot deck to tell Julius Caesar's fortune, and the ancient Egyptians called The Tarot (pronounced to rhyme with *sparrow*) The Book of Thoth. Some scholars even claim that the *Apocalypse*, the last book of the *New Testament*, applies the symbolism of The Tarot to prophecy. Tarot pictures are said to have adorned the walls of an ancient Egyptian Initiation Temple inside the Great Pyramid.

Whether or not The Tarot are really this old, they have been around for sure for at least 500 years. In the 14th century, they were used in Italy to play a game called *Tarocco* or *Tarocchi*. Where did those 14th-century Italians get the cards? Perhaps from wandering gypsies who brought them from Asia.

Where The Tarot came from doesn't matter as much as what these strange cards mean. In his poem, *The Wasteland* (Tarot cards often turn up in literature), T.S. Eliot called them, "a wicked pack of cards." But none of the designs on the cards are really wicked in themselves. The real power of these cards is the way they can help you to look at your problems and think out solutions. Each card is a symbol of an important part of life and living. If you lay the cards out, look at them and think about them, the sight of these symbols can sometimes trigger just the bit of buried information or memory you need to come up with the answer you seek.

Don't think that we're inviting you to psych yourself out on The Tarot. In this book, we hope to show you how to have fun with these odd picture cards. After all, for centuries people have used The Tarot to tell fortunes. And everyone's interested in their future, aren't they? (If they aren't, maybe they're at least curious about what the pictures on these cards are supposed to mean.)

A full Tarot deck consists of 78 cards, divided into two packs. Twenty-two of the cards are called the "Greater Trumps" or "The Major Arcana." (An *arcanum* is a mystery or secret.) The other 56 cards are known as the "Lesser Trumps" or "The Minor Arcana."

The Major Arcana are picture cards showing strange scenes and characters that may or may not mean what they seem to mean. The card known as "The Tower," for example, shows two men falling out of a lightning-blasted tower. Not surprisingly, this card stands for adversity, misery, catastrophe, blighted hope, and thwarted ambition.

On the other hand, the ugly demons grinning from the card known as "The Devil" aren't all bad. Among other things, this card tell you that "selfishness leads to loneliness and poverty," and "more is won through love than hate." You just can't leap to conclusions about the meanings of the cards in The Tarot.

The Minor Arcana or Lesser Trumps consist of four suits, like ordinary playing cards. But instead of hearts, diamonds, spades, and clubs, The Tarot suits are called *Pentacles* or *Stars* (money); *Cups* (love and emotion); *Swords* (ambition, force, courage, action); *Wands* (energy, growth, enterprise).

When you use The Tarot, remember that any card may have more than one meaning. Right side up, a card is likely to have a favorable meaning. Upside-down, or *reversed*, the card can become unlucky. For example, when the card known as "The Magician" is right side up it stands for willpower, wisdom, skill, and the correct use of power. But reversed, it means indecision and the use of power for destructive ends.

Before we tell you what each card means, we'll describe two different methods you can use to read The Tarot. There are many ways to read The Tarot, but whichever one you choose, remember that practice with the cards will give you skill. At first you will have to look up the meaning of each card you deal out, but in time you can learn to remember the meaning of each card.

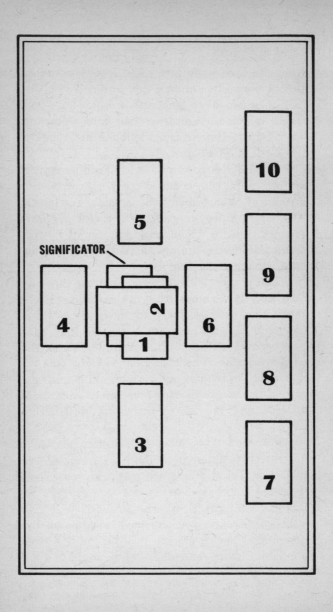

THE ANCIENT CELTIC METHOD

1. Choose a card to represent the *querent,* the one whose fortune is being told. If he or she is a young person with fair hair, you might choose the Page of Cups to represent him or her. If your querent is young and dark, use the Page of Pentacles. For a dark older woman, use the Queen of Cups; for a fair-haired older woman, choose the Queen of Wands. If the querent is a dark, older man, he may be represented by the King of Pentacles. A fair-haired older man can be symbolized by the King of Wands.

The card which represents the querent is called the *Significator.* Place it in the center, face up.

2. Ask the querent to shuffle the rest of the deck thoroughly. As he does so, he should concentrate on the question he wants The Tarot to to answer.

3. The querent should next cut the pack into three piles with the left hand, cutting toward the left.

4. The reader (the one who is telling the fortune) now picks up each pile and puts it on top of the next pile. This should be done with the left hand, toward the left. Cards should be face downward.

5. Turn over the top card, and put it over the *significator* card. This card shows the influences that are at work around your querent.

6. Turn over the next card and put it on its side over the first. This card will show what forces are working against the significator.

7. Turn up the third card and put it below the significator card. It will show something in the querent's past that is the basis of his problem.

8. Turn over the fourth card, and put it on the left of the significator card. This will show influences that are passing away.

9. Turn over the fifth card and put it above the significator card. This card represents a new influence that may shortly help or harm the querent.

10. Turn over the sixth card and put it on the right side of the significator. This shows what the querent may expect in the near future.

The cards are now arranged before you in the shape of a cross, with the significator card in the center, covered by the first and second cards. It is time to turn over the next four cards on the pile and arrange them in a straight line, one above the other, on the right side of the cross. Here is what these cards mean:

Seventh card: This shows the fears of the querent.

Eighth card: This shows the querent's environment, and the influences of his family and friends.

Ninth card: This shows the ambitions, desires, and hopes of the querent.

Tenth card: This is the last card, and it sums up the influence of all the other cards on the table. It should answer the querent's question and tell him what to expect to happen.

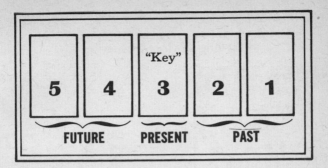

Quick-Answer Spread

All you need for this spread is five cards. Have the querent shuffle the cards thoroughly, and cut them into three packs as before, cutting to the left with the left hand. As he (or she) does this, the querent should concentrate on the question he wants answered.

After the cards have been cut, put the three piles together from the left, with the left hand. Now turn up five cards, putting them before you in a row, starting with card No. 1 at the right, card No. 2 at the left of No. 1, card No. 3 at the left of No. 2, etc.

Cards No. 1 and 2 represent the querent's past.

Cards No. 4 and 5 represent his future.

Card No. 3 is the "Key" card, and represents his present.

After reading the five cards, ask the querent to make a wish. If the majority of cards are right side up (from the reader's point of view), he will get his wish. If they are reversed, he won't.

THE MEANING OF THE CARDS

The Major Arcana

The Magician:

Right side up — mind over matter; be logical; solve your problems with your own skills and good sense. Use power for good. *Reversed* — indecision brings disaster; beware use of power for evil ends; restlessness leads to defeat; lack of persistence leaves you lacking.

The Fool:

Right side up — you have a choice, so make it the right one; keep the faith; give and you will receive. *Reversed* — your will is too weak; develop self-discipline or you will make the wrong choice; selfishness leads to suffering.

THE EMPRESS.

The Empress:

Right side up — wealth and good fortune for partnerships; harmony brings happiness; be fair to everyone and keep your emotional balance; loving vibrations attract love in return. *Reversed* — you could fritter away all your resources; poverty could hit home; bad vibes unless you stand by your decisions; you may have to learn to be happy alone.

THE EMPEROR.

The Emperor:

Right side up — a card of power for those who keep their cool; use power to help those who are weaker; be honest; rely on your creative energy and inner resources. *Reversed* — revenge is your undoing; jealousy and resentment leave you unrewarded; forgive and forget; cross at the green — accidents can happen.

The High
Priestess:

Right side up — hidden influences at work; mysterious forces of fate surround you; look beneath the surface of things; do what your heart tells you is right. *Reversed* — worry wears away the mind; don't take things at face value; conquer moodiness and don't be passive.

The Hierophant
(or High Priest):

Right side up — need to conform; work with the system; be optimistic and generous; good judgement brings happiness. *Reversed* — disregarding conventions will get you in trouble; be open to new ideas; curb extravagance and stick to necessities; you are too happy-go-lucky and impractical.

The Lovers:

Right side up — you have a choice between good things; choose the path that offers peace of mind; harmonize the inner and outer you; choice means taking responsibility; cooperate and be happy. *Reversed* — parents interfere; family quarrels; you could choose the wrong thing and suffer; stabilize your emotions.

The Chariot:

Right side up — a card of victory; success through use of intelligence; money problems can be conquered; you can win if you keep your aims on a high level. *Reversed* — your project could fail; dishonest victories will be found out; control your emotions or risk disaster.

Strength:

Right side up — real strength comes from the spirit; love is stronger than hate; overcome evil with good; forgive enemies; hidden forces are at work; face reality. *Reversed* — shirking duties brings discord; power can be abused; temptations are all around, reject them; fear can defeat you.

The Hermit:

Right side up — a wise person will give you profitable advice; you may go on a journey; be discreet, and avoid telling secrets; refuse to argue; experience brings knowledge. *Reversed* — so-called "friends" could cause trouble; things may not be what they seem; those who refuse to grow up find themselves in trouble.

WHEEL OF FORTUNE.

The Wheel of Fortune:

Right side up — a lucky card, but the luck will be unexpected; old ties break and new conditions take some getting used to; face change with courage; be patient instead of negative. *Reversed* — you will reap what you sow; there could be a turn for the worse; it's always darkest before the dawn; guard against discord and irritability.

Justice:

JUSTICE.

Right side up — give a little, get a little; be moderate in all things; law suits and legal matters turn out favorably; old, outworn ways of doing things should be eliminated; education is necessary if you want a well-balanced mind. *Reversed* — injustice and inequality; legal matters bring complications; worry attracts trouble to you; don't let things hang in the balance; every action brings a reaction; government regulations bar your way.

The Hanged Man:

Right side up — if you sacrifice yourself, your life could change for the better; give without thought of getting; don't let material things dominate your soul; forgive your enemies and suspend judgement; a pause in your life, wait it out. *Reversed* — an ego trip goes nowhere; wasted effort; if you're arrogant, expect to be disappointed; worry undermines your efforts.

Death:

Right side up — transformation and change; something torn down will be transformed and renewed; you come to a new door — knock!; you feel creative but expect strong competition; new viewpoints can show the way out of a blind alley. *Reversed* — stagnation, but it will pass; beware selfishness; look before you leap; but don't hesitate too long.

TEMPERANCE.

Temperance:

Right side up — work hard and you'll get results; you'll be reunited with the one you love; don't waste your time with quarrelsome people; work together in harmony. *Reversed* — people gang up on you and compete. You could lose; if you're too possessive, you'll scare the one you care for away; stubbornness keeps you from getting ahead.

The Devil:

THE DEVIL.

Right side up — more is won through love than hate; replace coldness with warmth; illness, violence, force, and dissension seem to have the upper hand; there's no magic way to overcome handicaps; the "bonds" you think tie you down could be imaginary. *Reversed* — religion can heal; spiritual understanding is possible now; selfishness leads to loneliness and poverty; think out the problem so you can be part of the solution.

The Tower:

Right side up — overthrow of way of life; conflict; catastrophe; disruption that could lead to enlightenment; selfishness brings about a fall; extravagance brings bankruptcy; fight for high principles; you reap what you sow. *Reversed* — you need courage in the face of oppression; be watchful to avert danger; wrongdoers could be imprisoned.

The Star:

Right side up — hope, truth, and faith; you'll get the help you need; your health will improve; positive thinking is really powerful; words count, so choose them carefully; a strong character helps overcome problems. *Reversed* — stubbornness limits your chances to win out; what you think is real may be only an illusion; how can you make friends when you're so pessimistic?; if you don't finish projects, others won't have confidence in you.

The Moon:

THE MOON.

Right side up — the one you love could be unlucky just now; if you feel hostile, you'll encourage secret enemies; choose your companions with care — some of your friends are false; find a better scene and get into it; hard work can make you forget your troubles, and keep you out of trouble. *Reversed* — if you try, you can turn a bad scene into a good one; use your common sense instead of your imagination just now; silence is golden.

The Sun:

THE SUN.

Right side up — happiness and joy; you achieve; studies bring success; simple things give pleasure; the more unselfish the love, the greater the rewards; a happy marriage. *Reversed* — future plans don't seem to work out; a broken engagement or loss of something else you value; take care of everything you prize.

Judgement:

Right side up — you are on the verge of an awakening and a new outlook; an end is also a beginning; broaden your mentality; make new friends; change and renewal. *Reversed* — possible loss of possessions; watch your health; weakness leads to fear; what you prize could turn out to be worthless.

The World:

Right side up — assured success is yours when you complete your task; people in authority give you their goodwill; what has been slowed down in your life will now begin to move; don't give up, your efforts will pay off. *Reversed* — people in power give you a bad time; fear of change keeps you in a rut; you're too stubborn, move in the direction of compromise; learn the lessons the other cards in this reading have to teach you.

The Minor Arcana

In many ways, The Minor Arcana resembles an ordinary deck of playing cards. In fact, our playing cards of today grew out of The Minor Arcana. The suit of *Wands* became Clubs; *Cups* became Hearts; *Swords* turned into Spades; and *Pentacles* became Diamonds.

When using The Tarot, some people prefer to use only The Major Arcana cards. But in our opinion, you will get more information if you use both The Minor and Major Arcana when laying out a fortune-telling spread.

Ace of Wands:

Right side up — you can begin something now and make it pay off. An inheritance might come your way. *Reversed* — your new project doesn't work out; what ought to bring you happiness, doesn't.

Two of Wands:

Right side up — promotions and success in work; science plays an important part in your life; if you have a problem, analyze it and get the solution; you're on top of the world right now. *Reversed* — suffering and sadness; others will try to rule you.

Three of Wands:

Right side up — someone successful in business will offer help; business gains through partnership, self-confidence; you get the better of enemies. *Reversed* — the help offered has too many strings attached; you're in for a disappointment.

Four of Wands:

Right side up — initiative brings you honor; romance is in the air; good vibes from people in authority; peace and prosperity. *Reversed* — things work out well if you don't let your tensions get in your way.

Five of Wands:

Right side up — competition brings out the best in you; struggle to get to the top; business success. *Reversed* — upsets in business or on the job; quarrels; agreements you thought you had with others could come unglued.

Six of Wands:

Right side up — balance work and play; use soft-sell when pushing projects; strife ends in victory; good news; lucky for those in art, music, or drama. *Reversed* — your enemy may be victorious; good things are delayed; seek moderation, avoid being too aggressive — especially at work.

Seven of Wands:

Right side up — don't rely on others now, you can hold your own; keep aims on high level; stiff competition, but keep the faith and win out. *Reversed* — indecision leads to worry and embarrassment.

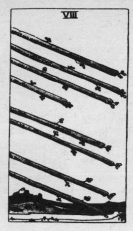

Eight of Wands:

Right side up — a journey will lead to a desired goal; a transfer might change things for you; rely on your own judgement and initiative for it will pay off; hope equals opportunity. *Reversed* — jealousy undermines self-confidence; quarrels at home; think before acting.

Nine of Wands:

Right side up — be prepared to be strong for a coming struggle; don't tell everything you know; good ideas are the best ammunition. *Reversed* — obstacles in your path delay you; arrogance brings displeasure from others; gossip could get you in trouble.

Ten of Wands:

Right side up — you'll soon solve your problem; the burden you're carrying won't slow you down; a change in status. *Reversed* — false friends and treachery; don't sue, you can't win; you could be separated from those you need.

PAGE of WANDS.

Page of Wands:

Right side up — blonde, blue-eyed young man or boy; someone who brings good news. (Can be used to represent blonde querent in card layout, either girl or boy.) *Reversed* — bad news; projects don't get started.

KNIGHT of WANDS.

Knight of Wands:

Right side up — Fair-haired man who stirs up quarrels, creates rivalry; card can also mean change of scene or going away. *Reversed* — quarrels that divide; someone is opposed to you and your interests.

QUEEN of WANDS.

Queen of Wands:

Right side up — a blonde, home-loving woman who is interested in your welfare; card also means success in whatever you undertake. *Reversed* — a strict, stingy woman; jealousy and deceit.

King of Wands:

Right side up — blonde, honest, and upright man; unexpected inheritance; happy marriage. *Reversed* — severe, unbending man; quarrels oppose you; someone offers good advice.

Ace of Cups:

Right side up — message from loved one; religion gives you a new and helpful outlook; travel to help others; joy. *Reversed* — moods get an emotional reaction; instability; misunderstood conversation; what was stable becomes unstable.

Two of Cups:

Right side up — a new friendship could lead to love; harmony from cooperation; emotions should be guided by reason. *Reversed* — false love; secrets come out into the open.

Three of Cups:

Right side up — things work out happily; old wounds heal; act to realize your ideals; you could have a prophetic dream. *Reversed* — lots of fun for everyone; keep enjoyment moderate.

Four of Cups:

Right side up — you're discontented with your present situation, but you're not ready to change it; are you sure you want what you're trying to get?; good things are in store for you; group activity is best. *Reversed* — a plot for revenge is revealed; investigate and get the truth; off with the old and on with the new.

Five of Cups:

Right side up — regret over loss; what you receive isn't as much as you expected; offers of fun have no appeal. *Reversed* — great expectations; an old friend reappears; lucky in love; a dream comes true.

Six of Cups:

Right side up — the past looks attractive now, but the future will be better; you could start all over with new friends and new surroundings. *Reversed* — a gift from the past; guard against shifts in loyalty; pay attention to hunches.

Seven of Cups:

Right side up — too many castles in the air can keep you earthbound; don't try to go in too many directions at once, but finish what you start. *Reversed* — thought and determination brings victory; truth is revealed; you get a chance to clear things up; contentment.

Eight of Cups:

Right side up — extravagance and self-sacrifice; the way things are aren't the way you want them to be; disappointment in love; too many family responsibilities for comfort. *Reversed* — good times coming; blend the practical with the ideal.

Nine of Cups:

Right side up — you get what you hoped for; satisfaction for the querent; good health and wise friends. *Reversed* — jealousy hurts; you make mistakes; watch your diet.

Ten of Cups:

Right side up — happy family life; friends are helpful; someone you cared for reenters your life. *Reversed* — you lose a friend; quarrels at home; too much emotional crossfire; old debts must be paid.

Page of Cups:

Right side up — young person with brown hair, hazel eyes; news of a new beginning; new methods affect a job. *Reversed* — obstacles crop up for you to stumble over; secrets can be revealed to embarrass you; those who deceive are found out.

KNIGHT ⚬ CUPS.

Knight of Cups:

Right side up — young man with brown hair, hazel eyes; bringer of thoughts of love and affection; messages or an invitation; you are offered propositions that could advance. *Reversed* — watch out for deceit; propositions may conceal fraud; rivalry.

QUEEN ⚬ CUPS.

Queen of Cups:

Right side up — woman with brown hair, hazel eyes; a happy marriage; gain through imagination. *Reversed* — a woman who seems fond of you may not have your good at heart; dishonesty; what you think is real may be illusion.

King of Cups:

Right side up — man with brown hair, hazel eyes; contact with business, law, or the ministry; a helpful friend; you benefit from someone's generosity. *Reversed* — loss through the law; a person with violent emotions means harm; someone's dishonesty hurts.

Ace of Swords:

Right side up — too much of everything; might is right; force results in conquest; struggle brings organization. *Reversed* — news of sickness or death; power can equal tyranny; news is bad or suppressed; mental blocks hamper you.

115

Two of Swords:

Right side up — new methods of working bring balance; hostility is suspended; too much "cool" chills romance; stalemates slow you down. *Reversed* — things start moving, but maybe in the wrong direction; stay out of bad company; possessions bring trouble; getting to the top won't be half the fun.

Three of Swords:

Right side up — separation, especially from loved ones; discord on the job; friends are quarrelsome; be more practical. *Reversed* — you could lose something you value; loss in a lawsuit; someone you've hurt brings confusion; antagonism leads to splitsville.

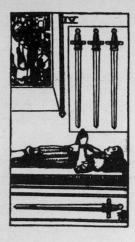

Four of Swords:

Right side up — get off by yourself and think things through; remorse in exile; recovery through positive thinking. *Reversed* — patience is rewarded; persist and win; keep cool although others are quarrelsome; give some, get some.

Five of Swords:

Right side up — guard yourself against danger; alertness pays off; faith overcomes obstacles; if you're right, don't give in. *Reversed* — quarrels end in loss; negative thinking can weaken you; sickness due to money worries; danger ahead.

Six of Swords:

Right side up — a way out of difficulties; keep trying, you'll get there; organize for success; help others now through your talents; journey by water. *Reversed* — if in trouble, you'll stay there; friends aren't very friendly; going in too many directions at once gets you nowhere; checking accounts don't check out.

Seven of Swords:

Right side up — sports and travel are dangerous now; plans may fail; coworkers gossip about you; someone may try to help himself to your property; watch out for pitfalls. *Reversed* — good times follow bad; concentrate on work and conditions may improve; good advice shows you how to win; a call to service.

Eight of Swords:

Right side up — you're boxed in and don't know which way is out; frustration; fear of failure; too much attention to petty details makes you neglect what's important. *Reversed* — a breakthrough; enthusiasm frees you from fear; new beginnings break old bonds.

Nine of Swords:

Right side up — propaganda can be a trap; confusion and doubt over an important matter; discord on the job; illness of a loved one; arguments waste energy. *Reversed* — confinement; quarrels make enemies; loss of reputation.

Ten of Swords:

Right side up — you could lose a job; lots of burdens to bear; you may be your own worst enemy. *Reversed* — good things happen, but they won't last; faith banishes discouragement; some gains, some losses; break bad habits.

PAGE of SWORDS.

Page of Swords:

Right side up — dark-haired, brown-eyed young person; watch out for trouble; you're on shaky ground so keep your eyes open. *Reversed* — unexpected events find you unprepared; someone steals a march on you when you aren't looking; all surprises aren't pleasant.

KNIGHT of SWORDS.

Knight of Swords:

Right side up — dark-haired, brown-eyed young man; domineering person; someone with courage helps you out; powerful forces line up for you if the cards on either side are good. *Reversed* — bragging and extravagance bring about a downfall; someone is plotting against you.

QUEEN of SWORDS.

Queen of Swords:

Right side up — dark-haired, brown-eyed woman; an acquaintance with sorrow; possible loss of a loved one. *Reversed* — way-out behavior will shock others; stand fast in the face of bigotry; meet intolerance with broad-mindedness.

121

King of Swords:

Right side up — dark-haired, brown-eyed man of power; ask advice of a wise man if you need help; a time of judgement. *Reversed* — don't expect justice or kindness just now; lawsuits will cost too much.

Ace of Pentacles:

Right side up — money from an artistic endeavor; social contacts bring gain; happiness and prosperity. *Reversed* — balance your budget or lose; money can bring corruption; waste of talents and riches.

Two of
Pentacles:

Right side up — gain through
ideas and partnerships; independence through hard work;
more responsibility, but you can
handle it. *Reversed* — you're
laughing on the outside, but cry-
ing on the inside; mental strain
from too much responsibility;
all work and no play chills romance.

Three of
Pentacles:

Right side up — a marriage for
money; your efforts pay off in
cash; success. *Reversed* — you
have to pay for mistakes; gossip
stirs up trouble; shoddy work-
manship increases costs.

Four of
Pentacles:

Right side up — profits from partners and friends; hold onto what you've got; an inheritance; possessions give you power, but don't be miserly. *Reversed* — arguments bring setbacks; loss of possessions; frustration because others oppose you.

Five of
Pentacles:

Right side up — money and friends vanish; if you think only about material things, you're poor indeed. *Reversed* — lucky in love; hidden influences help you out; belief should be backed up with facts.

Six of Pentacles:

Right side up — happiness in the family; share good things with others; cast your bread upon the waters. *Reversed* — stay out of bad company; too much spending brings debt; those you thought loyal may change their minds.

Seven of Pentacles:

Right side up — change of environment brings better conditions; sympathy and unselfishness pay off; it takes time, but hard work will bring you what you want. *Reversed* — worry over money; haste makes waste; correct misunderstandings; smooth out family quarrels.

Eight of
Pentacles:

Right side up — you must learn before you earn; a job is in your future if you have the training; build a foundation for your ideals. *Reversed* — goals set too high can't be reached; don't let your heart rule your head; misplaced emotion results in a lovers' quarrel; impressions are misleading.

Nine of
Pentacles:

Right side up — you'll get what you hope for; harmony at home; success in accomplishment; team up with one who is wise. *Reversed* — jealousy and bad faith bring loss; waste of resources; change for the worse at home.

Ten of
Pentacles:

Right side up — money to spend, perhaps through an inheritance; unusual friends bring unexpected gains; prosperity and good reputation. *Reversed* — emotional crossfire; misfortune through forgotten debts; sudden change in the home; stay away from project that could be a gamble.

Page of
Pentacles:

Right side up — dark-haired, black-eyed young person; someone brings news or new ideas; study brings rewards. *Reversed* — remorse after spending too much; the ideas of others don't agree with yours; a verdict could go against you.

KNIGHT of PENTACLES

Knight of
Pentacles:

Right side up — black-haired, black-eyed young man who could increase your prosperity; patient effort brings health and money gains; hard work and responsibility. *Reversed* — someone is trying to take advantage of you; too much idleness brings stagnation.

QUEEN of PENTACLES

Queen of
Pentacles:

Right side up — black-haired, black-eyed woman; good use of talents; freedom from fear. *Reversed* — fear and suspicion; duties neglected mean loss of independence.

King of
Pentacles:

Right side up — black-haired, black-eyed older man, successful in business; a member of the "Establishment" could have the answer to your problem. *Reversed* — gambling will put you behind the eight-ball; disaster if you use your talents to further harmful projects.

NUMEROLOGY – GETTING YOUR NUMBER

Numerology has been a numbers game since the long-ago days of the ancient Babylonians, Egyptians, and Hebrews. These sages of ancient times believed that each number contained vibrations that held the key to one's destiny. They also believed that every number had its counterpart in certain letters of the alphabet. The chart below will show you how this works:

1	2	3	4	5	6	7	8	9
A	B	C	D	E	F	G	H	I
J	K	L	M	N	O	P	Q	R
S	T	U	V	W	X	Y	Z	

How do others see you? What is your destiny? The letters of your name are supposed to provide clues, if you turn each letter into its corresponding number and then add up the figures. (Be sure to use the name that you are known by to others, the name by which you think of yourself. For example, if you were christened "Alexandra," but have never been called anything but "Sandy," use "Sandy.") Be sure to add in your last name numbers, and those of your middle name, if you use it often.

Here's the way to find your magic number. We'll use a well-known example first to get you started:

```
R   I   C   H   A   R   D   N   I   X   O   N
9 + 9 + 3 + 8 + 1 + 9 + 4 + 5 + 9 + 6 + 6 + 5 = 74
```

Now split 74 in two (Numerology only deals with numbers from 1 to 9). $7 + 4 = 11$. Since 11 is bigger than 9, we split it in two and add it — $1 + 1 = 2$. Mr. Nixon is a TWO. You can read about him in the following section, but first add up the letters of your own name and find your own magic number.

If you are a Number ONE — You like to be right out there in front, leading the parade. In fact, whatever the action is, you'll try to play a leading part. Others are likely to fall back and let you take over because you are not only self-reliant and self-possessed, but aggressive and daring.

ONE'S have lots of vitality, and the golden glow they radiate is the real thing because they are warm-hearted and generous with those they care about. But if rubbed the wrong way, they really turn off, becoming indifferent and even callous. They know their own worth and are proud of their achievements, and they should be for they take their responsibilities seriously — even to the point of doing more than their share. But they want all this power and drive to be recognized, and are happiest in positions of authority.

As a ONE, you'll have to learn to curb that love of authority — it could turn into arrogance. Give up the spotlight now and then so that others have a chance to shine. ONE'S know where they're going, all right, but getting there can be an ego trip. So tone down your vanity, and be careful that your independence doesn't become abrasive to others.

Compatible numbers — You are happiest with a loving number 6, or a quiet, reflective number 2. You don't always get along so well with those dreamy 9's, domineering 6's — and especially other number 1's. Two Numero Uno's equal a personality clash that could be a mini-war.

If you are a Number TWO — Emotional, changeable, sentimental — you're nice to have around until you let your feelings get hurt. Criticism tends to make you crawl into a shell to hide your hurt feelings. Try toughening up that thin skin — some criticism is deserved and can be constructive.

If you want a thing well done, ask a **TWO**. He may not talk up his good points — he may even put himself down. But he knows what you'll find out: There's no harder, more conscientious worker. Nor is there a better friend in need, or a stronger tower of strength in an emergency. What's more, they take the ups and downs of life in their stride.

TWO'S have good memories, and like to talk about old times. In fact, if they're not careful, they tend to live too much in the past, going on at a great rate about "the good old days" instead of changing with the times. They respect tradition and believe in carrying on tried-and-true customs and methods.

If you're a **TWO**, home and family mean a lot to you. You seek the security and safety that can only be found in love. Those you love are lucky, for **TWO'S** are sympathetic and loyal. The only drawback is that you tend to want to put a fence around people you care about. Don't be too possessive or dependent; it makes others feel smothered. Stand on your own feet, do your own thing — and let others do theirs.

Compatible numbers — Nobody understands you as well as another 2, but a 4 can balance your moodiness with a sense of stability. A 6 will respond to your romantic nature. Avoid those upsetting 7's. You won't get much help from 9 because you both are too inclined to dream away time in fantasy worlds.

If you are a Number THREE — Look for the life of the party — it's probably a **THREE**. You're witty, fun-loving, optimistic, outgoing — and maybe just a bit self-indulgent. Maybe you shouldn't try so hard to be so popular. You're generous and open-handed, but squandering time and money won't buy friendship. Your talents, charm, and luck will bring you all the friends you want — but don't take the good fortune that comes your way for granted. Everyone make their own luck.

One thing about **THREE'S**, they are honest, honorable souls — sometimes too much so. They are so frank and outspoken that simply saying what they think sometimes lands them in hot water. But along with their bluntness is a nature motivated by optimism. **THREE'S** think big. Fence them in, and they become bored and restless. They always have to be doing something, and hard work is often the weapon they use to fight boredom and make life interesting.

To be as popular and successful as they want to be, **THREE'S** should learn to curb their sharp tongues, and their hidden envy of others. Instead they should "think positive" so that their lively natures show to best advantage.

Compatible numbers — You're attracted to 1's and 8's, but their hot tempers will upset you.

You may find 5's good companions because you have many tastes in common. The most congenial friends of all will probably be 5's, while 4's can help you in business.

If you are a Number FOUR — You're practical, punctual, considerate of others. In fact, you are so dependable and duty-prone that at times it is just too much for you. There you are, in there pitching as hard as you can, and it seems nobody appreciates you. Maybe you've taken on so many burdens to carry that they can't even see you. Get others to share some of the load. Then they will not only get a taste of achievement, but they'll understand better what you're trying to do.

Your powers of concentration are deep and penetrating — in fact, you can become so wrapped up in what you're doing that you almost forget time and place. But you know exactly what you're doing, and your methods are painstaking and precise. You're also orderly in all you do — it's more efficient that way. Your mother never has to tell *you* to clean up your room! And no one should be surprised to find you hard at work in big clean-up campaigns — of crime, corruption, or community.

FOUR's are so hard-working that others might expect them to be dull, sober types. It isn't so. Get to know them, and they turn out to be witty, delightful company. They are born comedians when they want to be, and many FOUR'S keep audiences in stitches with their impressions of others.

Compatible numbers — Numbers 2 and 3 have good vibrations for 4's — they get along socially and have a lot in common. But 4's are often strongly attracted by 5's and 6's — sometimes to their sorrow. (A 5 can stir you up almost too much.) A 3 makes you more outgoing; a 7 will have plenty to talk about with you, and will provide you with needed ideas. An 8 is not too good for a 4 — too fiery.

If you are a Number FIVE — You do while others only dream. Sometimes you're almost too busy, tiring of projects before you complete them just so you can get on to the next one. Add a little method to all that mind power to get the results you want. Try planning ahead a little, even if it bores you.

You are quick-witted and fast-spoken. Novelty and change stimulate you, but oh how routine bores you. But try using a little routine on your boundless energy, concentrate so that your many skills work toward one goal.

FIVE'S like to live by their wits, and they keep their wits about them. Their heads rule their hearts most of the time. Logic instead of emotion — that's the rule of FIVE. All this clear-thinking makes them whizzes at bridging the communication gap. But it also tends to make them steer clear of getting personally involved with others. In fact, FIVE'S don't even like to discuss their personal life or yours. But as long as the subject is impersonal, they are terrific conversationalists.

Compatible numbers — Number 7 is as freedom-loving and adventurous as you are, but 3's you will find most harmonious. Number 6 people make good friends for you, and help tone down some of your wilder ideas. You're likely to feel hemmed in by 4's, but 7's expand your mind — even though they aren't much help when it comes to business. A 2 will go along with your moods.

If you are a Number SIX — Beauty and balance are your goals. Tactful and affectionate, you are a seeker of peace and harmony. Your disposition is warm and pleasant, and it attracts to you the companionship you crave.

Your talents probably lie in the artistic and creative field. Your outlook is idealistic and poetic. Those high standards you possess make you a solid, dependable citizen with a strong sense of fair play. But your love of harmony can make you shy away from arguments, even when you should take a stand for your own good. Sometimes you even redo someone else's sloppy work rather than hand out some deserved criticism. But let anyone threaten someone you love, and you come out fighting. You're protective of those near and dear — sometimes to the point of smother love.

Unlike most people, SIX'S have to learn to control their generous impulses. They are so sympathetic that they offer help even when it isn't needed. They idealize others, and all too often trust the wrong people. If you're a SIX, try to be more realistic. Don't assume that everyone is good hearted, trustworthy, and loyal.

Everything is at sixes and sevens when a SIX lets his emotions run away with him. Then impulses wins out over logic, and there's big trouble. Try to think before you act, SIX. Be less impulsive too in coming to quick decisions.

Compatible numbers — You are in seventh heaven with another 6, but a Number 9 friend will never let you down. You can look for help in business from 5's and 8's, and 5's also make good companions (as do 4's). A Number 9 friend can be a comfort and an encouragement when the going gets rough. You have to work harder to get along with 7's — they're too unpredictable for you.

If you are a Number SEVEN — You're a trend-setter and a born noncomformist. Freedom and independence of action are vital to you. You're progressive and liberal toward others in all that you do or say, for you have an idealistic nature that wants to better conditions. Liberty and equality are more than just words to you. You are willing to work hard to bring about reforms.

To some, you appear to be just a dreamer. Others might put you down as some kind of radical. That could be because you want to discard the old and replace it with what's new, and you want to do it now. Your ideas seem to come out of the blue, and you try to put them into practice before people are ready for them. Try to slow down those eccentric and erratic actions. Concentrate on working out ideas so that they make sense to others. Rebelliousness will get you nowhere, but it can make others think you are too impulsive and irresponsible.

"Conservatism" is a word you probably don't care for, but by being more conservative in your methods, you can become important socially —

and perhaps even politically. Many statesmen have been SEVEN'S. If you give your word, keep it. You should never promise anything you can't deliver — others will expect you to always live up to your own high standards.

SEVEN'S seem to be loners, for they aren't easy to know. The truth is, they're too shy to make friends easily — but once they do form a friendship, it's probably for keeps. They don't care for parties, gossip, or chitchat — but they are good listeners if you have something worthwhile to say. Their minds are usually on serious subjects — science (fiction and fact), religion, philosophy, and life's mysteries, such as the occult. They're seekers, searchers, devoted to the things they believe in.

Compatible numbers — Number 1's make congenial friends, and 4's and 9's are good business partners for a 7. You're inspired by 5's, and can get good financial advice from 3's and 4's. For scientific projects, 8's and 9's can help put your ideas to work and encourage your ambition.

If you are a Number EIGHT — You think big and expect big things to happen. And they probably do if you put your energy and enthusiasm behind them. In fact, all that you achieve, you achieve through action, drive, and determination. So aim high and choose lofty goals.

Adventure and excitment suit you, for you are fearless and daring. Although your emotions are fiery, you can be cool and alert in an emergency. But watch that quick temper. It is not to your advantage to fly off the handle. Try not to be too aggressive or argumentative. You'll get further faster if you learn to be more patient and tactful.

You're a born leader, and you're happy working for a cause that will help the unfortunate or oppressed. You can't be forced to do what you don't want to do, but no one is more generous and open-handed with time, energy, and money than an EIGHT. Nor does an EIGHT expect gratitude or payment for helping out. Being able to assist is reward enough.

EIGHT'S don't like to mix business and pleasure, but they put everything they've got into whatever they're doing. Sometimes, however, their strong wills and determination make them go to extremes in speech and action. This kind of "all-or-nothing" approach can lower their chances of success, for their aggressive spirit can antagonize others who might be helpful. You can move full speed ahead toward your goal, EIGHT, without steamrolling the opposition.

Compatible numbers — The sparkle of 6's turn you on because they share your zest for life. They will make you good companions and partners if you try to cooperate and harmonize with them. Your pioneering spirit makes you attractive to 5's, but other 8's will clash with you in a power struggle of violent proportions. Number 1's and 3's understand you, but don't get along easily with you.

If you are a Number NINE — Sensitive, perceptive — you really identify with the needs of other human beings. You are real humanitarians — almost too much so at times, for if you get wrapped up in some worthy cause you can put your friends and families way back in second place. But you do have the power to influence and guide people, so use it well. Live up to your ideals, or you will suffer from a sense of selfishness. Behave always in an honorable way, or you will lose the confidence and respect you inspire in others.

NINE'S seem to have keen intuition, and often are able to sense the feelings of others without being told. But when it comes to their own feelings, they can be moody, withdrawn, and secretive, leaving others wondering what's the matter. Then the next minute they may bounce back, almost bubbling with joy. The truth is, a NINE is unpredictable, except when it comes to his love for humanity. If a NINE should become rich, he is likely to give most of his wealth away to help others.

Unpredictability is the problem of NINE'S. They are independent and don't like to be pushed, but they can be easily swayed by an appeal to their symphathies. They don't like to quarrel, but they can explode into wrath if you don't share their concerns. They sometimes seem timid, but they crave power and can become very arrogant. They are deeply interested in all humanity, yet they can become very self-centered if they only daydream instead of work to bring out their best traits. They should devote themselves to helping others if they want to find inner peace.

Compatible numbers — No one will understand you as much as another 9, but no one will be more drawn to you than a number 8. Numbers 5's will be alert, lively friends; and Number 7's will admire and help you. For good business relations, look for Number 4's. Steer clear of proud, often ruthless 1's, and control your outburst around 3's.

Those who believe in numerology say that the numbers your name adds up to represent your personality, the way you appear to others. But they also claim that the numbers your birthdate adds up to show the real inner you. To find this "inner you" number take the number that represents the month you were born in, add it to the day you were born, and add the total to the last two numbers of the year of your birth. For example, if you were born February 4, 1959, you would add $2 + 4 + 59 = 65$, and then break the 65 in half, getting 6 + 5 = 11 — and then 1 + 1 = 2. Your name number, for example, might be an 8, giving you an 8 personality — but the true inner you would be a 2.

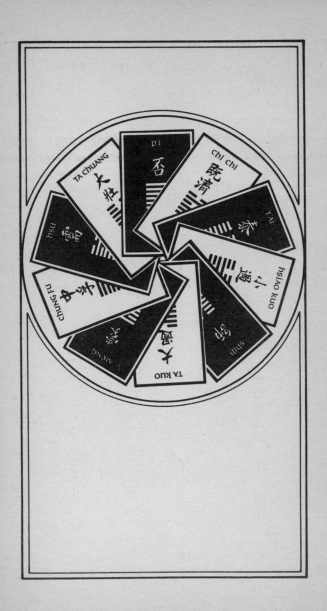

ASK THE I CHING

Decisions! Decisions! Sometimes it's hard to come up with the right answer. Can that answer you seek be found in a copy of the *I Ching* (pronounced "yee jing"), the ancient Chinese *Book of Change?*

The *I Ching* is nothing new. In fact, it is at least 3,000 years old. It is an ancient collection of wise sayings and helpful advice. The sayings are organized into 64 groups, and each group is represented by a certain hexagram (a six-line pattern). You ask a question, throw coins or black and white sticks to get a certain hexagram, and read the answer that goes with it.

Strictly speaking, the "answer" you get from the hexagram is not your "fortune" — that is, the *I Ching* does not predict the future. What it does do is point out what could happen if you do thus-and-so.

Confucius called the *I Ching* "the perfect book." This great Chinese teacher (551-479?) consulted his copy of the *I Ching* so often that he wore out its leather bindings three times. He said that if he had 50 years to spare, he would spend them all studying the *I Ching* so that he might "escape falling into great errors."

Carl Jung, the Swiss psychiatrist, believed that the *I Ching* helped solve problems by drawing the answer out of the user's subconscious (or unconscious) mind. The subconscious is that part of your mind that is active when you dream.

It is believed to be a storehouse of all your experiences. Somewhere in that storehouse might be just the information you need to help you make the right decisions. Jung saw the *I Ching* hexagrams as keys to unlock that mental storehouse.

Let's suppose you are wondering whether you ought to drop out of school and go to work. When you consult the *I Ching*, hexagram 39 turns up. In our "Table of Meanings" (see page 168), hexagram 39 says: "Overcoming obstacles helps to strengthen character. Follow the advice of a wise person." Of course, if you look hexagram 39 up in *The Book of Changes* itself, you will get more detailed advice. (Two good editions of the book are the one by Richard Wilhelm and Cary F. Baynes, published by Princeton University Press; and the paperback edition by John Blofeld, published by E.P. Dutton.)

If our quick answer in the "Table of Meanings" doesn't help you much, consult a copy of the *I Ching* for more advice. You will discover that each line of each hexagram has a meaning of its own. In the case of No. 39, the bottom line tells you to wait — not to make any snap decisions. The second line from the bottom (always read the hexagrams from the bottom up) urges you to seek advice from someone you respect and trust. The third line hints that if you follow the advice of lines 1 and 2, you will get an opportunity to be of service. Line 4 says that if you go ahead without seeking advice, you'll lose that opportunity and get into trouble. Line 5 assures you that a wise friend will come to give you advice you need. And the top or sixth line says that waiting for your friend's advice will bring you good luck.

Believers in the *I Ching* say that it has all the answers. But to find these answers, you will need a copy of the book (there are many paperbacks available); special wands or sticks, or just coins such as pennies or nickles.

If you decide to use wands, you can make your own. Take six popsickle sticks. Paint one side of each stick black. Paint the other side black on both ends and white in the middle — or just leave the center third of each stick unpainted. When the paint is dry, you are ready to consult the *I Ching*.

Write out your question or just concentrate strongly on it. Shuffle the sticks, holding them behind your back. Toss them onto the floor or a surface in front of you.

Now pick up the stick that is nearest to you. Place it in front of you. This stick will serve as the bottom of the hexagram you are going to form. Pick up the next nearest stick, and put it above the bottom one. Repeat until all six sticks are arranged in a compact rectangle in front of you.

To make it easier, you can find the number of the hexagram you have formed by consulting the "Table of Numbers" on the following pages. (It will save you the trouble of searching for it through the pages of the *I Ching*.) Just find the upper and lower trigrams (three-line patterns) and note the number in the box where the two columns bisect. For example, if the tri-

Upper Trigram→ Lower Trigram ↓	1 Ch'ien	4 Chên
1 Ch'ien	1	34
4 Chên	25	5
6 K'an	6	40
7 Kên	33	62
8 K'un	12	16
5 Sun	44	32
3 Li	13	55
2 Tui	10	54

K'an	7 Kên	8 K'un	5 Sun	3 Li	2 Tui
5	26	11	9	14	43
3	27	24	42	21	17
29	4	7	59	64	47
39	52	15	53	56	31
8	23	2	20	35	45
48	18	46	57	50	28
63	22	36	37	30	49
60	41	19	61	38	58

gram of the lower third of your hexagram turns out to be No. 6 — "K'an" — and the upper third looks like No. 8 — "K'un" — 6 and 8 bisect at "7" — and that's the number of your hexagram and your answer in the "Table of Meanings."

If you prefer, you can use three coins to find your hexagram. Take three coins of the same denomination (pennies, nickles, dimes, quarters). Give "heads" the value of 2, and "tails" the value of 3. Concentrating on your question, shake the coins in your cupped hands, toss them onto a flat surface, and add the value of the up-turned sides. For example, two "heads" and one "tail" would add up to 7. The sums 7 and 9 stand for a black line with a white center. The sums 6 and 8 stand for a solid black line. Toss the coins six times to get a hexagram, working from the bottom line up, and drawing the lines of the hexagram on a piece of paper as you go.

Sometimes the *I Ching* seems to behave in a willful, stubborn way, answering in riddles. But the fault may really be yours because you may have only half thought out your question. If you get a vague or confusing answer, restate your question and try again.

The more you use the *I Ching*, the less it will puzzle you. Often its answers are right to the point. One girl who had trouble staying on a diet asked the *I Ching* for advice. A toss of the wands turned up hexagram 53. "Hasty actions [dropping the diet?] are unwise," the hexagram told her, "Proceed gradually, step by step. Firmness of purpose will bring results."

Many people have compared the *I Ching* to a wise friend who has been everywhere and seen everything. Such a friend could be expected to give you good advice. But don't expect that advice to always be clear-cut. *The Book of Change* is full of metaphors and you'll have to do some thinking in order to apply those metaphors to your own situation. (We have tried to simplify many of the metaphors in our "Table of Answers.") For example, hexagram 30 is called "Li" which might be translated as "Flaming Beauty." Its text says "Raising cows — good fortune." But even if you have no cows, the hexagram can still apply to your problem. Cows are dependent creatures that must be cared for. The meaning you can extract from this hexagram is that good luck can come from looking after those weaker or less fortunate than yourself.

Even when you get a foreboding answer from the *I Ching*, the situation will be far from hopeless. The worst the book will tell you is to cool it, lie low, and let whatever trouble is coming pass over.

It is no accident that the *I Ching* is called *The Book of Changes*, for its answers are based on the changing nature of everything in the universe. Nothing is static, says the *I Ching*. All things are in a continual state of change — bad things as well as good.

How did the *I Ching* happen? Originally, it was a set of three books. The other two books were called the *Lien Shan* and the *Kwei Zang*. In 213 B.C., a royal decree ordered all written works burned in China — except the *I Ching* and some manuscripts written by the king's scholars. The other two companion volumes were thrown to the flames, but the *I Ching* is believed to have been spared because it had helped the ruler solve so many of his own problems.

During the early months of World War II, Japanese naval officers consulted the *I Ching* regularly. They claimed it gave them answers that helped them plan the strategy which won them so many victories at sea. But in 1942, the Japanese high command forbade consulting the *I Ching* because it was "old-fashioned superstition." Many Japanese blamed the defeats their navy suffered from 1942 until the end of the war on the loss of the *I Ching* as a guide. "If the people at the top had not been too 'modern' to consult *The Book of Changes*," said one Japanese officer, "all our earlier victories would not have been thrown away."

Does the present-day Chinese government consult the *I Ching?* Author John Blofeld suggests that they may. He points out that in 1962, Chinese Communist forces launched attacks on the border between India and Tibet. Their objective: to regain territories given India in 1914. But instead of swooping down on India, the powerful Chinese army hesitated, then withdrew. What stopped them?

Mr. Blofeld thinks it possible that the Chinese high command acted upon advice given in *The Book of Changes*. Perhaps they found their answer in hexagram 6, called "Sung," which stands for "Conflict." "Sung" warns: "Compromise with the situation instead of causing conflict." It implies that retreat is the best policy.

Perhaps the Chinese high command turned up hexagram 49. Line 3 of this hexagram warns: "To advance now would bring misfortune, and persistence would lead to trouble." Line 6 says that good fortune will come to those who stay where they are.

No matter how seriously some people take the *I Ching*, you can just relax and enjoy it. Consulting it may not make you luckier, richer, or more popular — but it certainly can't hurt. It is full of wise counsel that urges you to always choose good over evil, and to be moderate in all things. At the very least, it could show you how to develop your best qualities by helping you to make good choices instead of bad ones.

TABLE OF MEANINGS

Hexagram No.
and Name   *General Meaning*

1 (Ch'ien — "The
   Creative")

Patience and perseverance bring success.

2 (K'un — "The Receptive")

Conform to the situation. Accept assistance and guidance instead of leading the way. Find happiness through helping another.

3 (Chun — "Difficulty")

Do not seek new goals. Define and organize present goals. Ask others to help you through present difficulty, and it will pass.

4 (Mêng — "Youthful Immaturity")

Seek guidance from one who is wiser and more experienced.

5 (Hsu — "Waiting")

Face reality and be patient. Have a clear mind before making decisions. A journey is good.

6 (Sung — "Conflict")

Consult an impartial person. Meet your opponent halfway. Compromise instead of causing conflict.

7 (Shih — "The Army")

Anger and attack are a last resort. Stick only to a good cause, and the strength justice brings you will lead to a more enduring victory.

8 (Pi — "Unity")

Ask another question of the *I Ching* for a good omen. Unite with others who want the same thing you do. Aid each other unselfishly.

9 (Hsiao Ch'u —
   "Strength of the
   Small")

Adapt rather than act, for trouble is on the way. There are obstacles, but friendly persuasion helps.

10 (Lu —
   "Conduct")

Trouble is present, but good humor and good manners can win over even the worst-tempered.

11 (T'ai — "Peace")

Good people gain power and good fortune. Peace and harmony follow.

12 (P'i — "Standstill")

Look for trouble from evildoers. Withdraw in the face of disorder and confusion. Plan your next move instead of taking immediate action.

13 (T'ung Jen — "Brotherhood")

Seek inspiration from like-minded persons. Peaceful union with friends restores courage to the heart.

14 (Ta Yu —
"Great Pos-
sessions")

If you have much, you could gain more. Be modest, not greedy. Unselfish aims insure success.

15 (Ch'ien —
"Modesty")

Moderation brings balance and inner peace. Modesty brings success.

16 (Yü —
"Repose")

Enthusiasm helps you gain allies. Firmness meets with response. Be confident and gain peace of mind.

17 (Sui — "Following")

Adapt to changes in the situation. Persist in the path of good. If there's trouble, it's not your fault.

18 (Ku — "What Has Been Spoiled")

Ignorance and inattention lead to failure. Work to improve conditions. What has happened before will happen again.

19 (Lin — "Approach")

Make good use of your time. Progress while you can.

20 (Kuan — "Contemplation")

Sincerity gains you respect. Set a trustworthy example and live up to it.

21 (Shih Ho — "Biting Through")

Be adaptable and modest. Effort and work bring success. Good time for legal matters.

22 (P'i — "Harmony")

Keep your goals small, and you will have success. Rest and meditate. Contemplation will soothe you.

23 (Po — "Splitting Apart")

Avoid action. Lie low and keep cool. No advantage in seeking your goal. The weak flourish.

24 (Fu — "The Return")

No harm in going and coming, but have some goal. Examine your conscience before taking action.

25 (Wu Wang — "The Unexpected")

Maintain integrity. The evil meet with disaster. Help yourself by helping another. Sincere service brings rewards.

26 (Ta Ch'u —
"Holding
Firm")

The worthy gain respect. A journey is favored. Be firm in your convictions. Use the lessons you have learned.

27 (I — "Nourishment")

Give of yourself. Persistence brings good fortune. Be moderate in all you say and do.

28 (Ta Kuo —
"Excess")

The time is ripe for success. Take action with your conscience as your guide. Be sure your goal is a worthy one.

29 (K'an — "The
Abyss")

Danger! Remain true to yourself. Remain confident. Sincerity
helps you win.

30 (Li — "Flam-
ing Beauty")

Rewards if you care for those
weaker than yourself. There is
success ahead if you maintain
your persistence. Every purpose
has its time — and timing is
most important.

31 (Hsien —
"Attraction")

Opposites do well together. Seek
good advice and follow it. Keep
after what you want — you can
get it!

32 (Hêng — "Duration")

Freedom from error. Be firm of will while changing with the times. Have a goal in mind, for every end means a new beginning.

33 (Tun — "Retreat")

Withdraw from present situation with dignity. Avoid those who mean you no good. Yielding to those who have your good at heart can bring rewards.

34 (Ta Chuang — "Power of the Great")

Avoid arrogance and boasting. Be fair and just while dealing with obstacles.

35 (Chin — "Progress")

Progress is faster when the going is slow but sure. It is risky to try to rise too fast.

36 (Ming I — "The Light Darkens")

Be cautious and reserved. Things are difficult, but don't give up. Fix your will upon righteousness.

37 (Chia Jên — "The Family")

Actions speak louder than words. Those who have been held down should persist. Loyalty to loved ones brings happiness.

38 (K'uei —
   "Opposition")

There is a breakdown in communications. Work out misunderstanding with those you love. Good luck in small matters.

39 (Chien —
   "Trouble")

Need help? Go to the top. Overcoming obstacles builds character. Follow the advice of one in authority.

40 (Hsieh —
   "Release")

Pressures and tensions are easing. Difficulties are being resolved, but don't let that stop you from going forward.

41 (Sun —
"Decrease")

Be creative and make do with what you have. Simplicity is best. Loss leads to some gain.

42 (I — "In-
crease")

Don't be overbearing, but rid yourself of faults and evil impulses. Undertake a project of self-improvement.

43 (Kuai —
"Resolution")

Practice what you preach. Honesty *is* the best policy.

44 (Kou —
"Coming to
Meet")

Arrangements made now won't
last long. Beware of dishonesty
and ulterior motives. If you have
the upper hand, use it wisely.

45 (Ts'ui —
"Gathering
Together")

The time has come to give up
something for something more
important. Take precautions
against the unexpected. Fore-
warned is forearmed.

46 (Sheng —
"Pushing
Upward")

Consult an expert and banish
anxiety. Good advice will help.
Be adaptable. Effort brings success.

47 (K'un — "Adversity")

Obstacles are only temporary. Remain inwardly strong in the face of adversity. Something hidden causes trouble.

48 (Ching — "A Well")

Discriminate carefully between right and wrong. Work for the good of all, not just for yourself. Don't attempt the impossible.

49 (Ko — "Revolution")

Radical changes must fulfill a real need. Beware of being too hesitant or too hasty. Timing is important. If your cause is right, persist. You won't regret it.

50 (Ting — "The Caldron")

Some things can't be changed, so work on those that can. The wisdom of experience is nourishing.

51 (Chên — "Thunder")

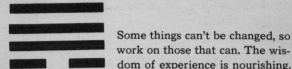

Disturbances shock us, but we should not postpone putting our lives in order. Use discipline on yourself, and you can overcome obstacles around you.

52 (Kên — "Keeping Still")

Don't worry without good cause. Keep your mind on your own situation, and don't make any abrupt changes.

172

53 (Chien —
"Gradual
Progress")

Hasty actions are unwise. Proceed gradually, step by step. Firmness of purpose will bring results.

54 (Kuei Mei —
"The Marry-
ing Maiden")

You and your partner haven't much in common. Do you belong together? Action is inadvisable.

55 (Fêng —
"Abundance")

Prosperity and progress. Don't be sad — your worries are illusions. Good things come.

56 (Lü — "The Wanderer")

Good luck in small things. But be careful and reserved if traveling. Courtesy and helpfulness earn you the goodwill of strangers.

57 (Sun — "Submission")

Progress is slow but sure — if your goals are clear. Someone important can be helpful. Give a little, get a little.

58 (Tui — "Joy")

If you are right, be happy. It is best now to appear gentle and compromising on the surface, but be firm and strong within. Don't put your trust in the unstable.

174

59 (Huan — "Dispersal")

Broaden your interests — banish selfishness. Success, if you unite with others for the common good.

60 (Chieh — "Restraint")

Be thrifty, but not too controlled. Discipline prevents things from falling apart, but maybe you should relax a little. Ease up.

61 (Chung Fu — "Integrity")

Keep yourself free from prejudice and open to the truth. You can influence others through sympathy and understanding.

62 (Hsiao Kuo — "Success of the Small")

You must walk before you can fly. Be content with modest success. The humble are favored over the mighty.

63 (Chi Chi — "After Completion")

Good luck at the start, not so good later. Pay attention to details and avert coming danger. Maintain balance.

64 (Wei Chi — "Before Completion")

Great responsibility, but it's hard to push toward your goal now. Act according to conscience.